Street Life and Prayer

One Woman's Journey from
25 Years of Alcohol and Drug Addiction to Freedom

Geraldine Thomas

To my parents, Mr. and Mrs. Frank and Jessie L. Tate.

To Sweet Sadie (better known as Mother Flora Mae
Thomas); Mr. Leroy Mikel;
And Mr. Jam.

To my sisters, Frankie L. Stevenson and Louise Ivey.

And most of all, I would like to thank God for giving me
the strength and courage to write this book
in spite of it all.

Disclaimer:

If someone reads this book and find some similarities don't panic, it is only a coincident.

Some text has been added, and some text has been taken away to protect the innocent.

Contents

Preface

This book came about after approximately twelve years of sobriety, and wanting to share what God had done for me. It was such a profound feeling that I felt there should be as many people as possible who should feel God's grace. When I discovered I could fall asleep at night and did not have to pass out, and could wake up in the morning and not have to come to, I knew who was in the bed next to me when I would wake up; oh, how grateful I was. What God did for me, He will do for anyone because we are all his children. All we have to do is ask, be serious, and be consistent about it. Don't give up because if you have the faith that God will heal you, it will happen. Don't believe that lie about "God won't dwell in an unclean temple" because it is written to come as you are with no preparation or appointments needed, to just seek Him and you will find, ask and you shall be granted.

The main reason I am writing this book is to tell everyone about how my twenty-five year journey of hard-core drug and alcohol addiction was conquered through prayer—lots and lots of prayer— and recovery. He might not come when you want Him to, but He is always on time. What an awesome God we serve. Hallelujah!

My Story
My Addiction
My Redemption

This book is about redemption. It is written to tell the world about how good God is, and no matter what you are going through or what you have done in your life, God will forgive you just for the asking.

It is never too late to ask God for forgiveness, and ask Him to heal your body. I am a living witness who can stand before you today and tell you that He can, and He will.

This book is about how being curious about drugs and alcohol will destroy you. It speaks about how, in order to be healed from any drug addiction, you must first take responsibility for your own actions and stop the blame game.

If you are not using drugs and alcohol, don't start because if you use it long enough, it will become a problem, a problem that you will not be able to handle on your own. If you are currently using, there is help; one must seek recovery and healing. So, people, please wake up and smell the coffee before it turns into tea because, believe me, it will.

Chapter 1

Watch for the Signs

This is a transcript for addicts and those that claim not to be addicts yet. Whether alcohol drinkers, cocaine users, pharmaceutical takers, marijuana smokers, heroin shooters, crystal meth users, or users of any type of drug that exists, there is hope and strength in this book for every sick and suffering addict. Some of the names and dates in this book have been changed to protect the innocent. This book is for all nationalities and genders. It is for everyone. No discrimination is involved in this book because that is one thing that drugs and alcohol does not do and that is discriminate.

This book was written for one purpose and one purpose only: to tell the truth, my truth, in hope that it will help and prevent others from experiencing the devastation I endured as well as my family. I know I received my healing from my higher power that I choose to call my Lord and Savior, Jesus Christ. You can have your own choice. This is mine. If by chance, someone benefits from this book, call it a blessing.

Let me tell you how wonderful my Higher Power is. He is good. He healed my body and my mind just by asking Him, and I was consistent in doing so. That's what He did for me, and I truly believe He will do the same for others who believe in Him.

Living as an addict to substance abuse can be very painful, heartbreaking, devastating, degrading, and more often than not, deadly.

The beginning of my drug addiction was what most would call "having a good time partying," not knowing my party would be a twenty-five-year run.

Here are a few *signs* that an upcoming drug addict and alcoholic should be aware of. When these signs show up, stop dead in your tracks and begin a spiritual cleansing because when these signs appear, you are about to be in some deep shit, take it from me.

Sign 1: The first thing to go is your telephone. Your life is about to be so messed up that you really don't want to talk to anyone who has any meaning in your life.

Sign 2: The freezer is nearly bare, and you wonder who ate all the meat, knowing all the time that you did not buy any meat because you spent most, if not all, of your money with the dope man. Sign 3: You find yourself at the Dollar Store buying candles, saying you just like the way they look and smell, knowing all the time you definitely were not going to pay the utility bill anyhow. Again,

here you go setting yourself up for another letdown.

Sign 4: A large amount of dirty clothes starts to pile up throughout your home. You then use the excuse that the clothes are piling up because you are not feeling well, knowing that is a lie. One thing addicts learn how to do better than anything else is lie. Sometimes it's the only way an addict can get their drug and alcohol. Lies do not hold up for very long. They will let you down in the middle of the streets while you are thinking of another lie to cover up for the previous lie. Lies that most of the time you can't even remember you told.

Sign 5: Dishes in the kitchen start to pile sky-high with hardened food on the plates. And when someone asks what's going on with the dishes, the reply is usually, "Well, the gas is off, and I don't have any hot water, so I'd just rather not deal with it." Then you go on to say, "What are you working with?" That is the cue that you don't want to talk about the dishes anymore, but you want to go on to bigger and better things, or so you thought.

Sign 6: You come out of the back room from using drugs and see one of your best road dogs and someone you've never seen before sitting on your sofa. You don't question who the new person is, what their name is, and where they live. None of the important things that a sane, sober-minded person would be concerned with, like knowing how this person could enter your home without your permission. This is a sign that you are now about to lose control over who comes in and out of your home. You are treading in deep water now. You just brush it off as if it's no big deal. This is just another sign that you are becoming more addicted to the substance you are using; you are losing control over your life.

When a person gets to this point, it's not too late to turn your life around and get some help! I had to stop acting as though I was in control. I had to admit to myself, and others, that I had lost control in order for my Higher Power to be able to intervene and rescue me. I needed that so badly.

Let me bring you up to date on how I arrived at this point in my life. One summer night in July 1972, I arrived in Los Angeles, California, on a large bus with my five-month-old son and five-year- old daughter. We were innocent people without a clue of what kind of horrible things awaited us in the trenches. When I first arrived in the big city, coming from a small town in the South—Mississippi—I was running from a very abusive man. I was searching, trying to make a better life for my children and myself.

Traveling to a strange place I had never been to in my life, I only knew five ladies in the entire city, and they were sisters. I had a telephone number for one of the sisters, but no address. After getting off the bus, it was very difficult to get down the escalators with two small children. I finally made it to the bottom floor where the cabs were waiting. On our way to the telephone booths, there were several men insisting they were going to give us a ride to where we needed to go whether we liked it or not. They were dressed flamboyantly, with long hair and long coats, making statements like "Can I give y'all a ride, baby?" My answer was "No, thank you." I answered very respectfully. Despite my dysfunctional upbringing, I did have manners.

My children and I kept right on walking without hesitation. When I spotted the long train of cabs that were waiting outside, that's when I hit my pockets and said, "Damn, I only have one dollar and fifty cents! How far will a cab take me with this?" I had a telephone number and no address. Before leaving Mississippi, I did not have time to call my friend's mother and get the new address. So I just took off with limited information. I called my friend's telephone number only to learn the number had been disconnected, and there was no new number. My heart sunk. After a few minutes, I made a collect call to Mississippi, to my friend's mother's home. She gave me my friend's address on Broadway Avenue in Los Angeles. I really lucked out to reach someone at that time of the morning. It was approximately 11:30 p.m. in Los Angeles; therefore, it was about 1:30 a.m. in Mississippi. Now the drama began. How was I going to get from downtown

Street Life and Prayer

Los Angeles to South Central on Broadway Avenue with one dollar and fifty cents in my pocket and with two minor children to care for whom I loved very much? Trying to get from the bus depot to my friend's home was very frustrating and scary. While in the bathroom changing my son's diaper—which I had to do quite often as he was suffering from diarrhea due to feeding him the readily prepared formula that we had been traveling with—I met the housekeeping aide who worked for the bus depot. This was when I received my first experience of coldness as she seemed very distant when I approached her. It made me remember an old saying: "Ain't no love in the heart of the city." She was mopping the bathroom floor. I spoke to her and asked her name. When she told me her name, I proceeded to tell her I had just arrived in Los Angeles from down South—Mississippi—and I only had one dollar and some change in my possession. I told her I had traveled very far with two minor children, and I needed a ride to my friend's house on Eighty-Seventh and Broadway. I explained that I did not have a telephone number to call to have someone pick me up because the only number I had for my friend had been disconnected, and there was no new number.

She looked at me and said, "Why don't you go outside and speak to the yellow-cab driver and ask him how much will he charge to take you to Eighty-Seventh and Broadway?"

I looked at that lady and wondered why she would ask such a question when I had just explained that I only had a dollar and some change in my possession.

Reluctantly, I walked outside and looked at the cab drivers. I then turned around and walked back inside to the bathroom.

The woman asked me, "Did you ask the cab driver how much he would charge?"

I said, "No, because if the cab driver would have quoted two dollars, I wouldn't be able to afford it." She smiled. That

15

puzzled me. I did not understand why she would smile when I was explaining to her how hurt and confused I was at that time. Then a tall, dark, handsome young man walked up.

He said, "Hello, ladies."

I spoke, and she kissed him. As clueless as I was at the age of twenty years old, it did not take a rocket scientist for me to realize that there was a connection between them. I then found out that he was the woman's husband. I had begun to tear up.

That's when he asked, "What is wrong?"

I began to explained that my children and I had just arrived here in Los Angeles. We had no family here, and I only had one telephone number, with less than two dollars in my possession. I needed a ride to my friend's home on Eighty-Seventh and Broadway. I told him that I stood before him because I fled from my hometown down in the Delta of the Deep South in Mississippi from an abusive relationship in search of finding a safe and secure home for my little children and myself.

He replied, "Sure, we will take you and your babies where you need to go." He turned and looked at his wife and said, "Sure we can, baby. We drive right by there on our way home. Isn't that right?"

She paused and slowly replied, "Well, yeah!" He then asked me, "Where is your luggage? Let's get them." I said, "You are looking at them, sir. This is all I have."

Two grocery bags stuffed with clothes. I believe it was about three changes for each one of my children. The wife was just getting off work. She worked the swing shift.

So the gentleman said, "Well, I guess we are just about ready to go, aren't we?"

We proceeded to get ready to leave. It was pitch-black outside once we drove out of the well-lit area of the bus depot. We drove on a freeway to go around a long turnpike; I had never seen anything like it before in my life. Although I had been to two other states, however, on that night, that turnpike ride seemed to be one of the loneliest rides I had ever taken in my life. The woman's husband played a tape by a black female singer who played piano. The title of the song that tore my heart into pieces was "You've Got a Friend." At that moment, I lost it. I cried so hard it was uncontrollable. All I could do was hold on to my daughter and hold my son in my lap. I cried so much that when I touched his blanket, it was wet with my tears. At that moment, I looked at my daughter and told her, "Baby, if we get one slice of bread, we must break it into three pieces."

She replied, "Yes, Mama." She looked at me and said, "Mommy, why are you crying? Don't cry! We are all right! Please don't cry!"

I am crying right now as I write this. That's how deep the wounds are. That's when I knew I had to get some strength and stop crying.

So I said, "Okay, baby. Mommy will not cry anymore." Right after that, she said, "Mommy, where are we going?"

I did not want to let her know that I was not sure. So I said, "To a friend's home, baby."

She said, "Okay, Mommy."

We continued driving to Eighty-Seventh and Broadway. When we arrived at my destination, the woman's husband told me, "I wish you and your family a long and happy life here in Los Angeles, California. I must say to you, please make your choices wisely because this is something that you have right now. It is your obligation to make the right decisions for yourself and your family, which I know you will."

I laughed. That was when my friend came to her front door and said, "Geraldine! Geraldine Thomas, is that you? Because there is no one else in this world that I know that laughs like that." She came out to the car and thanked the couple for getting me and my children to her home safely. I was very happy as well. I thanked them and went into my friend's home.

Chapter 2

A New Beginning for Me and My Family

After arriving at my friend's home on that warm summer night in the year of 1972, I had places I wanted to go, people I was going to meet, and things I was going to see and do. Things would happen in my life that I would not have ever imagined in a million years.

My friend gave my son her immediate attention, treating him as if he were her own. She had this big car that she loaded us all into, and we went to a doctor she knew would see my son because he was her children's doctor, and he was a good doctor. He took my word that when I became able, I would return to his office and make sure he was compensated for the good medical attention he gave my son. A few months later, I did just that. The doctor also made it possible for me to get my baby's medication as well. And for that, I was truly grateful.

After we left the doctor's office, we returned to my friend's home where she introduced me to her next-door neighbor, who just fell in love with my son. This lady would babysit him anytime I needed without any charge. I really appreciate all the kindness that she showed me and my family.

Due to the fact that I did not have a job, my friend's four sisters would pitch in and assist me in any way they could. I thanked them. After being in Los Angeles for two months, I met a young man.

His name was David, a friend of one of the sisters' husband. He and I became pretty close, I thought. He would do anything in his power to help my children and me with our expenses. David took me any place I needed to go. Although he had a job, he would make time for my appointments since I was new to Los Angeles. I had a lot of appointments to make. On the other hand, there was one lady who knew David before I arrived in Los Angeles, but she never paid him any attention until she discovered he was interested in my family and me.

One day, returning to my friend's home, when I walked upon the porch, she was kissing him with everything she had. At that moment, I came to the conclusion that David was not the man for me and my children. I felt that no harm was done because we had not been intimate with each other. I found it a little disappointing, but nothing that I could not handle. I had just ended an abusive relationship a few months earlier. That was one of the reasons I was in Los Angeles, so it was not difficult for me to move on.

At that time, I connected with one of my longtime childhood friends from back home in Mississippi. His name was Jordan. Jordan was a very good friend of mine, and there was never any hanky- panky with Jordan and I. We were just true childhood friends. Jordan was very kind, laughed all the time, and if you were his friend, he would do anything in his power to make sure you had any- and everything you needed. That evening, after the incident on the porch with the lady and David, Jordan came by the house where I was staying, and I told Jordan about the unpleasant scene I had witnessed.

Jordan said, "Don't worry, Geraldine, I will help you get through all of this."

Jordan lived in California five years before I arrived. He had three sisters and two brothers, who had been living in Los Angeles for many years before Jordan arrived. Therefore, he was pretty much established when we got here, so he was able to help me. Jordan was married with two beautiful children and a beautiful wife. To this day, I consider her my friend, although I don't see much of her. When they found out we were here in California, Jordan and his wife were very kind to my children and me.

Jordon said to me, "Geraldine, I know where another one of our friends live that you knew from back home, and I am going to let him know you are here so he can come by and see you and the children, if it's okay with you."

I said, "Sure, Jordon. But who are you talking about?" He said, "Jones."

My jaw dropped because Jones was one of our friends from back home that I always admired, and Jordan knew this. Later that evening, Jordan called me and asked if it was okay if he and Jones could come by to visit for a little while. I said, "Sure." I told Jordan I was wondering why it took so long for him to make this happen. A few days later, Jordan and Jones arrived. I was delighted to see the two of them together. It was a wonderful picture that I had not seen in a long time. I was instantly attracted to Jones, although I tried not to let it be known because that was the last thought I had about him the last time I saw him.

Three months after arriving in Los Angeles, I finally started looking for an apartment in the city. Jordan took me around from place to place in search of a home. It took about one week before I found this cute little apartment in South

Central L.A. that I just fell in love with. This would be my first apartment where I would be the head of my household. I was just ecstatic, overjoyed. I felt, for once in my life, that I was about to become the sole provider for me and my family which made me very happy. I was the sole provider, which made me very happy. The owner of the apartment building that I chose to move into her name was Mrs. Minnie. Mrs. Minnie lived in the complex as well. The apartment was a very well-kept six-unit building. There were three units downstairs and three units upstairs. She lived on the property in the first unit upstairs. She was a very nice lady.

I did not have any furniture for my first apartment, so Jordan told me not to worry about it. He took me to a furniture store in Huntington Park and cosigned for me to get a house full of new furniture, and trusted me to pay the monthly note until I paid it off. I kept my promise and paid it off on time. I never made a late payment. I always paid on time, and I was happy to be able to keep my word. I could get everything for my apartment except a stove and refrigerator. So it happened that Mrs. Minnie had a refrigerator in an empty apartment that was not in use and she sold it to me for fifty dollars. However, it was very much worth it, and I immediately accepted the offer. Jordan took me to a thrift store where I found a stove for seventy-five dollars, which I purchased. The stove was very clean and fairly new.

The apartment was a one-bedroom with hardwood floors and very clean. I was anxious to move in.

I had a feeling about myself that was unexplainable. It was such a tremendous feeling. I had been waiting to get this for such a long time, and it finally came true. I was happily the head of my household. The telephone company installed my telephone the day prior to my move-in date.

Jordan and his wife would often call and ask, "What do you guys need? How can we help? Are you okay?"

Jordan and his wife were very good friends of ours and were constantly assisting us in any way they could. I was very thankful for their friendship. Now I was moved into my new home, and my new life began. This was very good.

Jones and I began an intimate relationship after about six months of being friends again. It was okay until he decided to marry a woman with a good job, which I did not have. That's what tore us apart. My relationship with Jones was based on alcohol. We would never spend time together unless we were drinking. Our relationship was based on a bottle of whiskey and laughter. This was each and every time we were together. It seemed like the story of my life. Jones and I did a lot of wild things together, like riding his motorcycle on the freeway under the influence of alcohol while going from his home to mine. Maybe it was good that we did break up because we were living very dangerously.

This is another sign that one is in danger of becoming an alcoholic. When you are in a relationship and you only feel like you are a whole person or you only really enjoy your partner, and you can only express your thoughts and feelings when you are drunk, you need to take a closer look at yourself and your status as an alcoholic.

This is a very good sign that there could be a serious problem brewing, especially if one is drinking until one is beyond inebriation.

During the time when Jones would come over to visit, I met Carroll, my neighbor who lived downstairs, and she would babysit my children. After moving to South Central, Los Angeles, Carroll and I became very close friends. Carroll had three boys, and she was a single mother as well as a good homemaker and housekeeper. Her home was decorated in red and black. Whenever someone walked into Carroll's home, her guest would always comment on how nice and clean her home was. Not to be conceited, but my children and I also had a nice place. My apartment's decor colors were gold and brown, which meshed well with my shiny hardwood floors. Carroll's mother, Julia, lived up front in a big white house. Julia was strict with her grandsons, and that made them rebellious.

One evening, we all were sitting on Carroll's front porch drinking beer, and Carroll's middle son, Tray, had gotten so angry with his grandmother, Julia, that he went into the house, got a container of lighter fluid used for barbecue grills, and poured it into his grandmother's can of beer. He was very slick in doing so; he carefully caught us off guard. Neither one of us saw him do this. When Julia started to take a drink from her can of beer, the fluid was so strong it made her sick. We would not have known today who did it if he hadn't admitted it. Julia asked Tray why he did such a mean thing.

He said, "Because you are too controlling, and I cannot stand you."

That was a heavy blow for Tray's grandmother, to the point that she could not punish him at that moment. Her only reply was "I am so disappointed in you, Tray. I will deal with you later after my anger has eased."

That was the end of our partying for that day, which was something we did practically daily.

Carroll had many male friends who would call and come by her house practically every night during the week as well as on the weekend, but there was a very strict rule of thumb: you could not come by Carroll's home unless you brought a bag consisting of plenty of alcoholic beverages, cigarettes, and snacks for the adults and the children, and there must be more money left over in order for someone to return to the store if necessary. That went on for a very long time, for months, until I landed a job as a maid at an elegant hotel in 1974. There I met a charming young man who was so nice to me. He bought me gifts and anything else my little heart desired. He would do these nice things for me with no strings attached. I think that's what made me fall for him.

His name was Taylor. He was a big-boned dark man who wore eyeglasses. He walked with a limp on his left side and had a receding hairline, but he was quite handsome, and I truly adored him. I was happy to go to work because although we had a nice apartment and were living a good life, all I was doing was waking up every morning, getting my daughter dressed and off to school then getting my little baby bathed and dressed, cleaning up my apartment, and getting ready for the party to begin.

Carroll and I were the true making of two devoted alcoholics. There were no drugs involved at that time. However, now that I have a clear mind, I do believe alcohol drinking that went on from 1972 to 1974 was a great contributor to my heavy drug use and abuse. I would suggest to anyone whose life revolves around heavy drinking and partying, day in and day out, that they should take a long, hard look at their lives and try to turn it around before it is too late.

When Taylor and I hooked up, it was one of the best things that happened to me because together we moved from South Central to West Los Angeles. I had a few jobs in between time, but nothing outstanding. Taylor and I landed a two-bedroom apartment. That's when my children could have their own bedroom for the first time since we arrived in Los Angeles. Taylor and I both held down two jobs at the same time; therefore, we did not have any time to get involved with any of our neighbors. Today, I realize that it was a really good thing. As I entered the building where I lived, I noticed there were mostly single mothers who lived in that building, struggling from day to day but were still partying.

What I mean by "still partying" is that almost everyone in that building used some form of drug or another. At the time, I was what they called a "square" because all I was doing was drinking a classy scotch as well as a well-known gin after work—and on weekends only, which was the extent of my getting "high."

Taylor had a problem with some of the women in the building. When he came from work, they would be in the hallway of the building having a conversation, wearing lingerie, and flirting with every young man who passed their way.

Taylor would come into the apartment, tired and ready to eat. On the days I did not have to work, which were very seldom, he would say, "Honey, do you know our neighbors who are always out there in the hallway? Honey, I don't want to start any trouble, but every time I come into this building, those ladies, at least one, will have some type of question to ask me. Will you please ask them if they have any questions for this family to please address you with them and not me? Because I don't want any trouble out of their men, and I definitely sho' 'nough don't want any trouble out of you concerning those women."

I replied, "Honey, don't you worry yourself. I promise I will take care of it. You did the right thing to tell me about this situation. I'll handle it." And I did.

One month later, Honey and I were spending some quiet time together one evening. In our peaceful home, we had just finished a wonderful dinner, and we just kicked back, sharing some wonderful thoughts with each other. He was embracing me, and I was embracing him; we were just enjoying each other, if you know what I mean. We were so peaceful.

I met an elderly lady who lived in the same complex. I took a liking to her. She went to church all the time, and I trusted her with my children. So that particular evening, my babies were with this wonderful elderly lady. Therefore, we were all alone, which was very seldom. So we took full advantage of that particular night, and I mean full advantage. All of a sudden, Honey said, "Thanks, honey."

"For what?"

"Those ladies don't bother me anymore, and I know it is because you took care of it."

"How do you know I took care of it?"

"I can tell by the way they look at me when I walk into the building."

"You are right. I did take care of it. And I want you to promise me something. If you ever have any problem like that or similar, don't hesitate. Please let me know."

"I will, honey." On that note, we fell asleep very fulfilled. Oh, what a night! I really loved that man. He was one of the best things that happened to me since I arrived in Los Angeles. We were living really well for poor folks. We did not have a lot, but we never had to worry about how we were going to pay a bill or how we were going to put food on the table or how we were going to clothe the children. We had all those avenues covered. We lived like that for a few years and were doing really well. I drove a 1969 Buick Skylark. My Skylark was in mint condition; it ran well, just like new. Honey drove a 1974 brown-and- beige Dodge Charger. In 1976, Honey drove our family down south to my home in Mississippi. Taylor met all my family and everyone fell in love with him. My mom fell in love with Taylor. He was just that type of guy, and he loved her and the rest of my family as well.

I got a chance to see the young man that I fled from. I did not know how that would go, but believe it or not, it went okay. Some of the animosity had ceased.

Honey spent most of his vacation with my mother. I took him out a few times, but Taylor mostly wanted to stay home with my mom. He would tell me, "You go ahead. Go out with your sisters. I'll stay with your mom. I'll be okay."

We spent two weeks in Mississippi. Then we had to return to work. So we made our way back to the city, which was about time. Two weeks was plenty.

Oh, yes, on our way down south, we were stopped by a cop about one thirty in the morning for speeding. And for that, we had to go back about thirty miles, and they had to wake up a judge so he could fine us three hundred dollars before we could continue on our trip. We were told we had better be glad they could get a judge up; otherwise, we would have had to spend the night in that town until morning. We got out of there at about four o'clock that next morning, and about three hundred dollars shorter than we were when we started out. We made it back to Los Angeles in one piece and got back on track.

Taylor and I lived together as a couple, and we were very happy. This was in 1976. So in 1979, Taylor and I decided that we would get him a new car. I felt he was deserving of it. I was still happy with my 1969 Buick Skylark. I did not want a new car. I was okay with the one I had. However, by Taylor being the head of the household, we felt he needed and deserved to get a new car. So we pooled our money together, as most happy families would do, and went down to the dealership on Wilshire Boulevard. We picked out a 1979 Dodge Charger. As you can tell, the Charger was one of his favorite cars. The car was very pretty. It was steel gray and burgundy. The body was gray with half vinyl burgundy top with black interior. It rode nicely. Honey was pleased, and so was I because what made him happy made me happy, for the most part. I'm not saying we did not have our little ups and downs because that's not so, but it wasn't anything we could not work through.

Then it came time for our next vacation. We took one about every three years, which we felt was sufficient. This time, Honey decided I should take a flight home, and he would drive to Atlanta, Georgia, which was his home. Taylor hadn't been home in ten years; he told me so when we met. I agreed that could be a plan. That would work for me for one reason: I wanted him to be able to drive his new car home and show it off since he hadn't been home in ten years. Yes! Go for it! I loved it when a plan comes together, and that seemed like a good plan to me. So it came time for me to leave for my vacation. I packed everything up for my babies and myself about a week ahead of time so on the night before our flight was due to leave, I would have plenty of time to spend with my honey before we would fly off to Mississippi. It happened just like I had planned it. The last night Honey and I spent together before I left for my hometown was magnificent.

Our flight was due to leave that following morning. On our way to the airport, we were laughing, talking, and saying how much we loved each other. It was just beautiful. When it came time forme to board the plane, all I could remember saying was "I love you, and I will see you in two weeks. When I return, you will be able to drive your new car home."

We flew off into the sunset, our minds at ease. We had a two- hour layover in Tennessee, which was all right, because we were only a few minutes from Mississippi. We arrived home that evening. My dad and sisters met us at the airport and drove us home. The first thing my mom asked me after giving me a big hug and kiss was "Baby, how is Honey?"

I said, "He is fine! He is just waiting for us to return home, I had a great big smile on my face I was so happy."

Remember now, it had been three years since I had seen them. It was a happy reunion. Moving right along, my family and I had a good time for the most part, but when the two weeks were up, I was ready to get back to Los Angeles and get back to my honey. So late that Friday evening, my family took me to the airport, and my babies and I flew back to California without a hitch. When we arrived in Los Angeles, I could not wait to see my big baby. And when I did, I just fell into his arms with great relief and melted like a stick of butter that had landed on a hot stove. Honey welcomed the children back home. So we proceeded to drive home very happy. Now it came time for Honey to drive to Atlanta, Georgia. However, before that happened, I wanted to let him know how much I loved and missed him, which I did.

Sunday night came, and I made sure Honey had everything he needed, so most of what he needed was packed, and ready to go. Monday morning came, and Honey was ready to drive off into the sunset. I can only tell you how much I missed him. Two weeks passed, and Honey returned home. However, when Honey returned home, I felt as though he took something from our home here in Los Angeles and somehow left it in Georgia. He did not return the same way he left. Something was missing, but I did not know what. I just knew it was something. He was very quiet. I wanted to know how he enjoyed his vacation, and he was very short in answering. He started to come to bed late; before this vacation, he was the first one in bed and wanted to know how long it would be before I came to bed. Honey seemed very distant to the point that I could not reach him. I was concerned at this point, but I did not want to jump to conclusions. I was trying to figure this situation out. What was the best way for me to approach this?

One Saturday morning, I drove the Charger to the grocery store. After I finished grocery shopping, I made an effort to put the groceries in the trunk of Honey's car. That's when I discovered that Taylor's clothes were still in the car, unpacked. It was then that lights came on, dimmers went to blinking, and antenna went up. All kind of shit started going on in my head. I did not know what to think. All I knew was that "Something in the milk wasn't white." The reason I went to the store alone in the first place was to fix Honey a special birthday dinner with champagne and the whole nine yards. Normally, I did not drive Honey's car, as I said earlier. I was very happy driving my Skylark. Honey had keys to my car, and I had keys to his. We were a family. That's the way it was from the beginning. That particular morning, I decided to drive the Dodge, and that was when the shit hit the fan. I opened a big can of worms that morning, and that was not my intention at all. I was not aware that he had not unpacked because we had this large walk-in closet in our bedroom. Half was Honey's and half was mine. I am not the type of woman to ramble through my man's belongings because I did not feel I needed to. Although we shared the same bedroom, I felt there is still a certain amount of privacy a person is entitled to. I would give him that because I wanted the same in return. So I made it back from the store in one piece, although I didn't know how because I was in a daze driving home. I made it into the house with the groceries; I did not say anything about the unpacked clothes in the beginning.

After I put the groceries away, I said, "Honey, I drove the Charger to the store this morning."

He jumped straight up and said, "You did?"

I said, "Yes." At this time, I was afraid. I was shaking, afraid of what I didn't know. I was afraid of the unknown. Taylor said, "Honey, sit down please. I need to talk to you." At this time, he knew I had seen the unpacked clothes in his car that had been there for a little longer than a week. I said to myself, "Oh man, here we go." Remember now, Taylor and I had been together since 1974. Now it was 1979. He was all I knew as far as a mate. I had been true to him ever since we had been together. No swaying, no swagging, true to this man. Now it was time for me to hear what he had to say.

He began by saying, "Honey, you know I love you, don't you? Ever since we have been together, I have never been with no other woman but you. You do believe me, don't you?" I replied, "Yes, I believe you because I have never been with another man but you since we been together."

Taylor said, "Honey, I want you to know that you mean the world to me."

I said, "Likewise, I feel the same way about you." Then I said, "Wait a minute, Honey, why are you telling me all of this now?"

He said, "Honey, telling you this is not easy for me."

I screamed, "What is not easy? You are telling me all of this in order to tell me what?" He hesitated, and I said, "Please, tell me what you are talking about!"

He said, "Okay, you remember I told you I have not been home in ten years?"

I said, "I remember!"

Then he said, "But I did not tell you everything! Honey, I have a wife and three children. And while I was home, I got a chance to spend some time with them, and I really enjoyed myself. My wife lives alone with my son and my two daughters, and I promised them that I would return back to California and tie up some loose ends, and that I would return to Atlanta and try to be a husband to my wife and a father to my three children, something I had never been. I hope you can forgive me, but my plans are to move back to Atlanta, Georgia. My son needs me."

I was speechless. I was blown away. I was devastated. That was the worst pain I had ever felt in my life, coming from one individual. When I was able to speak again, I said, "I am just loose ends now?"

He said, "I was not referring to you as loose ends."

I said, "So where do me and my children fit in? Not to sound selfish, but what about us?"

He said, "Honey, one thing I do know is you are a strong black woman. I know you and the children will be all right."

I was not angry. I was hurt, devastated, blown away, feeling lost and surprised, and I blamed myself. At that time, I thought about how I would fill this void. I tried to think of all the roles that Taylor played in our lives. What was I going to do to cover his role? The reason I was not angry was because he did not have to tell me; however, I preferred that he told me the truth rather than stay with me and my babies while wanting to be someplace else. When I was able to speak, after I snapped out of my "comatose" state, I tried to see if we could fix this. You must remember I gave up everything for Taylor. I had given up all my friends and all my outside activities. I did not associate with anyone but him. If it did not involve Taylor, it did not involve me. He was my world. He fulfilled me.

When I was able to talk, I said to him, "Taylor, do you have to leave us? Is there any way we can take care of the children together from here and remain a family?"

Taylor's reply to that plea was "Honey, we might be able to take care of the children from here, but we cannot take care of the wife from here."

That's when I broke down, and I lost it. I cried so hard until I could not see. I could not see anything but the thought of being left all alone. After I regained my composure, I cleared my throat, dried my eyes, and said, "When do you plan to leave, Taylor?"

He said, "Well, I really had not set a date, but due to the fact that I have told you as much as I have this morning, I think it would be best if I leave now."

I replied, "I agree. I think it would be best if you leave today as well."

He said, "Okay."

I said to him, "I don't want to be here while you pack. So what I am going to do now is, I am going to go across the street to the pharmacy and pick up a few things that I really don't need right now, just to give you some time to pack in peace." I went on to say, "I am not going to hurry back. I am going to take my time. You may take anything that belongs to you, but nothing of mine. And I would appreciate it if you are gone when I get back."

He said, "I will be gone." And he also said, "Honey, I hope you will find it in your heart to forgive me. I am sorry our relationship had to end this way."

I said, "I am, too."

As I write this portion of my story, I am playing this blues song "I Found a Love," and right now, I am crying. That's how painful rethinking this portion of my life is.

I left and went across the street to the pharmacy. I must have walked every aisle in that store and spent at least twenty minutes in each aisle until I thought he had enough time to be gone. As I drove back into the back gate of our complex, Honey was driving out. As we passed each other, he blew his horn and I blew mine. I thought to myself, *Oh well. I got to start all over again.* And that is not easy, especially when you are starting from scratch. I mean, nothing but the grace of God would get me through this, and grace was all I had and that's all I needed, but I really did not know this at that time. I knew about the Lord, but at that time, I was not thinking logically. I was unable to return to work for two weeks. I had this slamming bar in my home that was stocked with anything you wanted to drink, and for two weeks, I turned to that bar for help, which was the wrong thing to do. I put my faith in something that could not help me.

One thing I was still doing through all of this was getting up every morning, getting my children dressed and off to school, and then I would start drinking again. I did that for two weeks straight, not thinking, just drinking. I was drinking to try to keep from thinking, which was again a bad choice. I woke up one morning, and I looked in the mirror. I was shocked at how bad I looked.

I said to myself, "I got to shake this." The bills were coming in, the cupboards were getting bare, and my children needed things. I said, "I got to get out of here. I got to go back to work. This isn't going to cut it."

I finally pulled myself together and returned to work. Upon returning to work, I guess I was not my old self. One of my male coworkers asked me, "Geraldine, what is the matter?"

When that question was asked, I could not hold back the tears. I broke down and ran downstairs to the women's locker room. I stayed in that locker room until I composed myself. When I finally got it together, I came out of the locker room to return to my workstation. The man had stopped what he was doing, and he was waiting on me to come out of the break room. That man, whom I will call Mr. Jam at this time, Mr. Jam said, "I guess this is my opportunity to tell you. Baby, you don't have a problem that we cannot fix together."

At that time, Mr. Jam was about twenty years older than I was, but this was the first time in many years that a man had spoken to me with the same sincerity that Honey spoke to me on the first time he and I met. When I heard Mr. Jam that morning, there was something about that statement that struck my heart. As they say, "You cannot hear until you can hear." That morning, I heard.

I had been talking to Mr. Jam for a long time, but itwas always about the job, nothing else. But somehow, that morning, he knew I needed more than just a conversation about the job. Two months later, I got my look back. We started dating, and it turned out to be a really good thing. He was a take-charge man, and that's what I needed at that time. Mr. Jam was a blues man, and I loved the blues as well. That was just one thing we had in common, among many other things. He liked good food, good drinks, and good times. He also liked taking care of his woman, and I liked taking care of my man. So we clicked. We started spending a lot of time together. He would always make sure my children and I had everything we needed. As you know, from what I said in the beginning of this book,

this is something that I like: a man who is good to me and my babies; this is one of the ways to my heart. So Mr. Jam and I rocked on in a good way.

Three months later, I received a collect call. Guess from whom. Lo and behold, it was Honey. I accepted the call long enough to tell him, "If you want to talk on this phone, you must dial direct."

He called right back, crying the blues. He said, "Honey, this is not working out like I thought it would. The woman is not right. The children are out of control. She lied to me. She is seeing somebody else. Honey, can I please come back home?"

I said, "Honey, as much as I would like to say yes, come on home, I can't because I am involved with another man now, and this man is good to my children and me. And due to the way he came into my life, I cannot see myself telling him I can't see him anymore because you are coming back home. I don't think that would be right. All I can say to you at this time is I am sorry it turned out this way for you. I hope you can forgive me, but at this time, I must say no. I wish you the best, but I must hang up now. Take care of yourself, good-bye, and good luck."

That was the last time I spoke with Honey. Mr. Jam and I continued to rock on in a good way.

Six months later, I received a call from one of my sisters telling me that my mother passed away from complications of diabetes, and she wanted to know when I would be coming home. I told her I would be leaving in about two days and to just give me enough time to get my job and my house in order since I had no one to take care of it while I was gone. She said, "Okay." I contacted Mr. Jam and told him I had lost my mother to complications of diabetes. He said, "I am sorry to hear this. When do you all want to leave?"

I said, "As soon as possible."

He said, "As soon as I hang up from you, I will call the airport and make the reservations for you all. As soon as you all are ready, let me know, and I will take you to the airport. Don't worry about the tickets. They will be round trip."

I said, "Thank you, Jam."

He replied, "You are welcome. I wish I could do more."

I said, "You have done aplenty." I got things together as much as possible, and I flew out two days later. I stayed for one month then returned home. The plan was to stay for two weeks, but my father asked me to stay longer. He said, "Please stay a little while longer because when you come back home again, you might be coming back to my funeral."

I said, "Dad, don't talk like that."

He said, "That is the way I feel, baby! I feel like my best friend is gone."

Sure enough, that was August 1979. I returned to Los Angeles and started our life over again. I was working in a hospital in the linen control department. So everything was going as usual. The children were going to school, and I was going to work every day, just living a normal life. Then that second dreaded telephone call came through. This was in December 1979.

My sister said, "Geraldine, Dad just passed away. When will you be home?"

I said, "In about two days after I get things together here." This was four months after we buried Mom. I called Mr. Jam and said, "Jam, my dad has gone on as well."

He said, "When do you want to leave?" I said, "As soon as possible."

He said, "We will do it the same way we did for your mom. No problem."

I said thank you, and one more time, I flew off to Mississippi, stayed for approximately two weeks, and returned to California. By this time, I was burned out with pain. I felt rather empty with a heavy burden on my shoulders. I was confused, and I didn't know which way to go. I knew, but I wasn't practicing it. I should have turned to the Lord, but I didn't. Because in the situation I was in, I was such an easy target for Satan to slip in on me; I should have been praying, asking the Lord for help. But I wasn't. I turned to my neighbors, the same people I had made a promise to stay away from. This was one of the biggest mistakes I'd ever made in my entire life. After that last trip to Mississippi, I let my guard down and went against my belief, which was to never use drugs. I began to visit my neighbors, and I took my first hit of marijuana—the biggest mistake I ever made in my life. That became a regular thing that I did, not realizing I was sinking deeper and deeper into my addiction. My addiction took me to a point where every time I would take a hit of marijuana, I would need to go outside. I did not know that this was a result of my getting high. I just knew that eventually, after taking a hit, I would seem to need some fresh air.

When Honey and I were together, we visited this couple who did not live too far from us. The husband will be called Winston. Winston was from Atlanta, Georgia. He and Honey grew up together. So we would visit their home and have dinner every now and then, and they would come to our home. So one night, after hitting some of that marijuana, I went on my usual trip outside in front of the apartments to get some fresh air, and who walked by? Winston! It had been over a year since I had seen Winston. The first question out of my mouth was "How have you and your family been? And when was the last time you heard from Honey? And how is he doing?"

Winston said, "You haven't heard? Honey took a bad bout with diabetes, and they had to amputate both of his legs up to his waist due to gangrene."

I said, "No shit." I was really sorry to hear that because after all that was said and done, Honey and I, despite everything, had some very good history between us. That took me for a spill. So I told Winston it was very nice seeing him again and for him to tell his family I said hello. Then I went back inside and continued doing what I had been doing night after night for a few months, getting high, which had become a routine.

As I continued going outside on my fresh-air binges, I would see this young man who would be standing outside a few apartments down from where I lived. He always stood on his top step. He was one of the best-looking men I had ever seen in my entire life. He had everything; I did not see anything missing. I will call him Mr. T. He was a fine man. At that time, we would just speak casually, nothing heavy. Then I would go back inside.

While all this was going on, my two children would be at home with everything they needed. I would prepare everything for them before I would go on my little journey. I would instruct them not to open the door for anyone. I would tell them that I was going to visit for a little while, and I would be back to check on them very shortly. They were cool with this. They would say, "Okay, Mama. We all right."

Off I would go. By this time, my addiction had gotten worse. I was just thinking that this was how it was, not knowing the consequences that this was going to bring me further down the road. I was young and dumb, didn't have a clue. I didn't know anything about life in the big city, and I had no one to inform me because everyone around me was getting high. When you surround yourself with negativity, you get negative results in return. There is an old saying that goes like this: *If you want to know who a person is and what they are about, all you need to do is check out who their friends are.*

Out of all those people who were in that apartment, not one said, "Geraldine, you go home. You don't need to be here. You have a nice home, a nice car, a good job, and two wonderful children. You don't need to be doing this. Go home and get yourself together. Get your life back in order and carry on as you have been doing for the last five years."

Not one of them said that to me. Do you know why? Because I was a good contributor. A group of drug addicts do not want to lose a good contributor. *Contributors* are people who put money in the drug pot to score the drugs. They were all guttersnippers.

Eventually, that young man who lived a few apartments down from me, who would stand outside, somehow made his way into my apartment one night, and we had a wonderful time. We thought that would just be a one-time thing, so he went his way and I went mine.

Then I met this guy who would bring my marijuana to me. I will call him Justin. He was one of those groupies who would hang out where I was getting high also. He spotted me in the crowd and took me to be a good thing. That's what I would call it today. So he gave me an alternative to how I was getting my drugs.

He said, "Geraldine, why are you hanging with the groupies and spending all of that money when I can just bring you your own sack to your apartment, and you will be able to get high in the privacy of your own home?"

I thought for a minute and said, "Yes, you are right." *Why don't I get my own sack?* People, people, this is a big sign. Wake up! When you stop chipping in with others and you begin to want to spend your money and buy your own drugs, you are on your way to becoming an independent drug addict. So now I was doing it another way. Now I would wait until my children went to sleep, then I would pull my own sack out. But this one thing did not change: I continued to have to eventually go outside sometime during the night. I would go outside and get some fresh air.

Winston was a cook at a restaurant not too far from my apartment complex. It had been about, oh, I'll say nine months since I had last seen Winston. So during my escape to the outside, who walked by? None other than Winston! So we spoke, and again I asked how he and his family had been doing, and how was Honey. This was when he told me.

He said, "You know, Geraldine, Honey passed away about two months ago."

I almost fell to the ground, and again I said, "No shit!" Winston said, "No shit."

Honey was gone; that blew me away. Instead of that sad news about Honey making me want to change my life, that gave me an excuse to want something a little stronger than marijuana to get high on, and what was floating in the neighborhood at that time was powdered cocaine. That was another big mistake I made. I called Justin up and asked him if he knew where I could score some powdered cocaine. Justin told me it was not a problem, and he had some on him right then. I asked how much he wanted for it, and he said nothing; it was free.

I said, "Okay, bring it over."

People, people, wake up! When a person agrees to give you a drug as expensive as powdered cocaine was back then, as a matter of fact, *any* drug for free, you need to run like hell because there is a catch-22 in the making. Nothing in the drug department is free— now or ever has been. There is a price you must pay one way or the other. If you don't want to pay the price, people, please stay away from alcohol and drugs.

Chapter 3

God Bless the Child Who Has His Own

Justin and I became really close, to the point that Mr. Jam and I began to drift apart. Between Mr. Jam's woman who knew the color of the sheets that were on his bed and Justin, my drugs, and me, I did not know which way to turn; I was totally confused. It doesn't take much to get a person confused when the person is an alcoholic and a drug addict.

People, I made some of my biggest mistakes during my addiction, larger than any sober individual could ever imagine. I am going to tell you more about the mistakes that I made as you read further in this book. Most of my regrettable mistakes were made during my drug addiction. I declared that no one would ever know about these instances in my life but God, the person who was involved, and I. I promised my children would never know. I promised myself that.

However, as I travel down these roads, highways, and byways, I see people walking with no direction, no substance, no hope, and no idea they can be healed. I feel it is my duty as a healed and recovering alcoholic and drug addict to do something for these people who are children of God.

I wrote this book to say, no matter who you are or what you have done in life to yourself or others, there is a God, and He will forgive you and heal your mind and body because He is in the miracle- working business. God healed me; He healed my mind and body. If He did it for me, He will do it for you just for the asking. You must be consistent to expect these miracles because that is what He does. He is in the miracle-working business. These things that I am going to tell you about that happened in my drug-addicted life are very degrading, embarrassing, and devastating, and I am very remorseful about these acts. However, in spite of it all, God still healed me, so I feel that I was healed for a reason, and I should not be selfish with my miracle. I need to share God's goodness with others who don't know about it. I would hope that some people will read this book before they get to the point I was at, and never get involved with alcohol, and drugs. That is one of my goals of writing this book. Another reason for writing this book is to let those who are already involved with drugs and alcohol know that one does not have to live the rest of their lives as a practicing alcoholic and drug addict. God will heal them. I am talking from experience, not what anyone told me. I am talking about what I know.

So Justin and I started going pretty steady because at that time, I was still working, making decent money, I had my own place and was independent.

Furthermore, by this time, Mr. Jam would take me out to lavish restaurants and clubs. I was so tied up in the drug scene I really could not concentrate on anything; all I could think about was getting back to Justin's or my own apartment so I could blow some smoke in the air. That was all I could think about, not where I was or who I was with, just the drugs.

People, wake up! This is not good! This is another sign you are not in control of your life anymore. The drug has taken over your life. When you reach this stage of your alcohol and drug addiction, this is where—before you lose everything—you should seek some help. Start with God, get some drug counseling, and seek a drug program. They *do* work. There is help, but you must seek it out. You will not hear this from your drug-club members; you must seek people who are in the recovery business. The guttersnippers are not going to tell you any information that will help you. Let me be clear: they do not want to lose good contributors who are making the drug club work, as I mentioned earlier on in this book. Please, please, if you are not using drugs, don't start; and if you are, seek some help before it is too late. I cannot express this enough.

At this point, I let one of my hometown female friends, and her two children move into my home. I will call her Sandra. I was still involved with Mr. Jam and Justin. Mr. Jam was very good to me; he had given me my own automobile gas card so I could purchase gas, tires, and whatever I needed for my car. I never knew the amount of the monthly statement. The statement was mailed to Mr. Jam's home. I did not know how blessed I was until I had lost that man; he was the first one to tell me, "Geraldine, you are on the wrong track. You need to leave those drugs alone before you destroy yourself and everything you stand for. Please, baby, leave the drugs alone."

Mr. Jam told me that plenty of times, but I was too far gone to turn around when he found out what I was going through. Every time we got together after I got hooked on drugs, he would plead with me. He would say, "Baby, if not for me, if not for yourself, please do it for your little children. Leave the drugs alone." Mr. Jam would faithfully tell me this. At that time in my life, I did not want to hear anything that had to do with leaving the drugs alone. Where I could get some more, maybe, but not "leave the drugs alone." I was hooked. So instead of leaving the drugs alone, I felt it would be better for everyone involved to leave Mr. Jam alone—the best friend I had. Justin and the drugs had me so blind I could not see the forest for the trees.

So one night, I went to Mr. Jam's home and told him, "Jam, I hope you will be able to forgive me. You are too nice to me for me to keep this charade going. I got to tell you what I have been doing."

He said, "Whatever you have to tell me, Geraldine, it can't be anything we cannot work through."

I said, "Yes it is, Jam."

He replied, "But promise me you will allow us to talk about it before we come to any decision."

I said, "Baby, the decision has already been made." I took the automobile gas card out of my purse and placed it on his bed.

He said, "Geraldine, this is a mistake. You don't mean this."

With tears rolling down my face, I said, "Baby, what is really so bad about this situation is that I know this is a mistake. All the other times I did not know I was making mistakes, but that time I knew. But, baby, I am too far gone to do anything about the situation, which is … I am involved with another man, and I don't want to do you wrong. Please forgive me."

I turned, and I walked away. I got into my car, and I drove off. I cried all the way home because I knew that the man had nothing but the best interest for my babies and me. I knew I was destroying a great relationship, and I did not have the strength to prevent it because Justin had been putting pressure on me, telling me it had to be him or Mr. Jam, and I couldn't have both. Justin even threatened to leave me if I did not hurry up and tell Mr. Jam we were an item.

Now as I look back on my life, it wasn't the fact that I was about to lose Justin. I realize today, the main reason I broke off one of the best relationships I ever had in my life was because of the drugs.

So I made it back to my apartment and called Justin and told him what I had done.

When I first met Justin, he had a wife and seven children. One day, during one of our visits, he told me his wife had moved out, taken the children, and he did not know why she moved or where she moved. Being a sick, suffering addict, my heart went out to him about what he had lost.

Justin lived in the apartment building next to the building that I lived in. I met Justin at one of the drug parties, and to me, he was just another groupie until he came up with this big, bright idea of me having my drugs all to myself, and he would supply them for me for a fair price. By this time, Sandra and her family had settled in, and she had the run of the house. Now that I had an adult there with my children, I was really drug chasing and hanging out with Justin. Justin and I started staying upstairs at his apartment, getting high most of the time. The drugs got so good to me that I thought it was Justin having that effect. Now that I look back on my life, I can see just how sick I really was; I was ill, and I did not know how to fix it. One day, I was at Justin's apartment, and his wife came into the apartment with her own door key. I was there alone; Justin had just made a run to go and get some more narcotics. I was waiting on pins and needles for him to return, so when the door opened, I thought it was him, but it wasn't; it was his wife. I was startled; therefore, I reacted very nervously.

She said, "No, baby, don't be bothered about me being here. The only reason I am here is to pick up something that I left behind. The only reason I came in is that I did not see his car outside. My advice to you is to get up and get everything you have and run like hell because this man is crazy." She got her shit and left, and she was on her way out of the door when she looked back at me and said, "Good luck, because you damn sure going to need it."

Everything was going really well. Justin called his mother down in his home state and told her about me, how good I was to him, and how well we got along. In front of me, he was giving this good report on our relationship; but in the back of my mind, I was still thinking about what his wife had told me during the conversation we had. Somehow, I could not get it out of my thoughts, but my love for Justin and the drugs would not allow me to handle it properly. I couldn't just get the hell out of there because I was too far gone to turn around. Instead, I kept going to Justin's home day in and day out like clockwork. It got to the point where I started spending more time at Justin's house than I did at my own.

So one night, Justin and I were spending some quiet time together at his home, and in the process, he said to me, "Geraldine, let's move in together so we can be together always. You know how I feel about you. It could only work out for the better for all four of us."

He was referring to my two babies when he said the four of us, of course. I was so in love with Justin and the drugs until it did not take much to convince me. So I told him, "Yes, I guess you might be right. It does make sense."

So I went back to my apartment. My housemate, Sandra, was asleep. I went into her room, the room that used to be my children's room. I gave it to her and her two children after she fell upon hard times and needed a place to stay. I told Sandra that I just left Justin's apartment, that he was asking me to move in with him, and I asked her what she thought about this. And I also asked Sandra what she thought about me allowing her to take over my apartment. I could see the expression on her face change with gratification. Sandra said, "If you feel like this is what you really want to do, it would be okay with me."

I told her I would think about it for a few days, and if everything worked out all right, then we will move forward with this plan. Sandra agreed. So I went into my bedroom I shared with my two children, and slept on it.

When I woke up, my mind was already made up. That's how strong my love was for Justin—and the drugs. This was on a Saturday morning; therefore, I had to wait until Monday morning to take care of my business with the apartment manager in the business office. I could hardly wait; I was anxious to get this process started. I spent the rest of the weekend with Justin, making plans to move in as soon as possible. First thing Monday morning, I was in the manager's office, asking if I could sign over my apartment lease to Sandra, my longtime friend, to allow me to move in with Justin. You should have seen the expression on her face. She was blown away. She could not believe what was coming out of my mouth.

Mrs. Jenkins, the apartment manager, said, "Geraldine, please, please do not leave your own apartment and move in with that man. You will be making the mistake of a lifetime. Please don't do this. That man is crazy. You see his wife and children recently left him. Do you think they left because she was so in love, and they were so very happy? No, it was because they were afraid of Justin. That man is crazy. Please don't do this."

I did not listen to her. I continued asking her the same favor over and over until she eventually gave in and said okay. She told me she thought this was a big mistake. I thanked Mrs. Jenkins, but I told her I was going to take my chances. I loved this man to the point that I was willing to risk this, and I hoped this move would turn out all right.

Mrs. Jenkins said, "It is okay to allow your longtime friend to take over your apartment, if you really want this. Just bring your friend into the office, so we can get the paperwork taken care of."

I thanked Mrs. Jenkins. Mrs. Jenkins said, "I really hope this works out for you, especially for your little children. Geraldine, Justin has to bring you into the office as well and put in a request to put your name on his lease, and then we can move forward with these transactions."

I agreed to this. I rushed back to my apartment with all the joy in the world. I was so happy that Mrs. Jenkins had given me the okay. I could not wait to tell Sandra the good news that Mrs. Jenkins had said it was okay for her to take over my apartment that my children and I had rented for years. The following day, Justin and I went to the apartment manager's office and completed the paperwork so I could move from one apartment to the next. The following day, Sandra and I went to the apartment manager's office where I signed my apartment over to her. This turned out to be one of the biggest mistakes I ever made in my life. I proceeded to move out of my longtime home. Sandra went and got her furniture out of storage and moved it into the apartment that I had so foolishly signed over to her.

Everything went very beautiful for about six months. After six months, the happiness and joy was short lived. One Friday at lunchtime, approximately six months after Justin and I moved in together, being the lovebird that I was, I decided to take Justin a surprise lunch; Justin was off work that day because he was scheduled to work the weekend. It was my payday, so I figured that it would be a nice gesture to do something nice for the man I loved. I decided to purchase some Chinese food and surprise Justin with a hot lunch. Upon my arrival at my home,

I discovered that Justin was not home. So I looked out in the back of the apartment complex and saw that Justin's car was parked out there. Therefore, I knew he was in the area. At this time, I was still friends with the ladies in the other building that I had just moved out of, or so I thought. So I walked to the next building where I used to live, to a friend's apartment, to ask her if she had seen Justin. The reason I went to her home was because I knew she worked swing shift, and I knew she would be home that time of day. I knocked, and the door eased open to the point that I could look right down the hall. I made two steps inside of her apartment. I began to call for Sabrina, my so-called friend.

I could see Justin and Sabrina walking down the hall, looking very surprised.

I said, "Hello." Justin said with anger in his voice, "What are you doing home this time of day?"

My reply was "I came to bring you your lunch, some of that Chinese food that you liked so much." Justin rudely thanked me; I told him that he was welcome. I told him I was going to head back to work because, after all, I was only on my lunch break. I then told them to have a nice day, and I turned and walked out of Sabrina's apartment. I did not go back to our apartment. I walked straight to my car on the busy street that I lived on, got into my car, made a U-turn in the middle of the street, went a few blocks down and took the freeway, and went straight back to work without having any lunch myself. I was very, very hurt and confused, dare I say. Remember now, it had only been about six months since I had turned my apartment over to my longtime, childhood friend and her two children and moved in with Justin.

I worked that afternoon without being able to concentrate on anything but what I saw on my lunch break. I got off work that evening and went straight home. On Fridays, I usually would stop off and pick up some drugs on my payday, but that Friday, I did not. I got off work, picked up a few things for my children, and I went straight home. When I arrived home, my children were there. They never would go outside after school until after I arrived home from work, and they asked, "Mama, can we go outside and play now that you are home?"

I would say yes, and they would at that time go outside. My children and I continued to have a close relationship even after we moved in with Justin.

I was sitting on the sofa in the living room watching TV, having a drink, when Justin walked in the house. I became very nervous for no reason. Later, I discovered why I got very nervous when he walked in the house. He went into the bedroom, put his bag down, went and used the restroom, went into the kitchen and got a drink of water. During all this time, he never did speak to me. I continued to be very nervous. After Justin finished all of these things, he came into the living room and said, "You think you are smart, don't you."

I said, "What are you talking about Justin?"

Justin then said, "I am going to show you who the boss is around here," and he hit me right in the face without any warning. He continued to beat me for about thirty minutes. Justin beat me from the living room to the bedroom and on into the bathroom where he grabbed my head and drove it straight into the bathroom window. Justin broke that bathroom window with my head. The windowpane was about two inches thick, and a piece of glass from that broken window that was as thin as a nail was sticking straight up behind my ear. It was about three inches long, and it never cut me. That had to be nothing but by the grace of God.

People, people, wake up! Don't be crazy when someone offers you good advice about someone or something. Most of the time, we know good advice when we hear it; some of us just don't want to face reality. Most of the time, we do not want to face reality because it can cause us a whole lot of pain. Wake up, people. Don't let this happen to you! I'm sharing these stories with you so you won't have to go through the pain and shame like I did. There are so many regrets that I have about how I lived my life, but if, by writing this book, I can help at least one person to not go through the hell and disgrace that I have gone through, then it will be well worth airing out my dirty laundry because so many went through what I went through and did not live to talk about it.

People, please, if you have not gotten involved with drugs and alcohol, please don't. If you are involved and you are still alive, it is not too late to turn your life around. My Higher Power, whom I wish to call God, did it for me; and I know if I could get healed, you can too. All you have to do is go to your Higher Power and just be consistent in asking, and He will do it for you because, after all, I do believe there is only one God. People, people, if you have your own place to live—I don't care if it's a matchbox—if it is yours, don't give your place up to move in with anyone. Ninety-nine percent of the time, it will be a big mistake, and eventually, one that will come back and bite you right where it hurts. Some will live through it, and some won't. It depends on who will be there to pick up the pieces because, believe me, the pieces will fall.

After Justin had beaten me for approximately thirty minutes, my little son came into the apartment and saw what was happening. He grabbed Justin's leg and started screaming, "Leave my mommy alone! Stop, Justin, stop!" And the only thing that stopped Justin was when my son said, "Justin, if I was a man, I would kill you right now!"

Justin then said, "Boy, you be quiet and go into your room and sit down!"

My son said, "You must be crazy, Justin!" My son ran back outside. When he came back into the apartment, he came back with my daughter, and my daughter jumped on Justin's back. She was beating him with one hand and holding on with the other hand, and then all three of us were fighting with Justin. Justin stopped beating me. After about two or three minutes had gone by, he went into the bedroom, and I immediately called the police. They came and arrested Justin because my eye was almost closed from the swelling. People, people, wake up! Can you imagine the guilt I would have carried, on top of all the guilt that I have today, if anything had happened to my children because of my selfishness? I was only thinking about me, me, me, and my love for the drugs. I was not thinking about what type of situation I was taking my little children into.

People, if you are in a situation similar to this, think about your little children, look at the big picture, play the tape all the way through, don't make your move too soon, and don't be selfish with your decision because the outcome can be devastating. What made the situation worse, the woman I saw Justin with, coming out of her bedroom earlier that day, who lived next door, could hear everything from her kitchen window. She was screaming, "Stop it, Justin, you leave her alone!"

That really made my blood boil, but it was my own fault because I knew Justin's wife and children had recently left him. My apartment manager had warned me not to give up my apartment to my longtime childhood friend and not to move in with Justin. But I did not listen. I moved; I had acted on feelings, not on logic, which was another big mistake I made.

After the police left, I got my two little children, went out, got into my car, and drove myself to the hospital. I knew I was hurt as I sat there at the hospital with my two little children.

There are no words that can explain the hurt, shame, and disgust that I felt toward myself and Justin. All I could do as I waited to be seen was to go into the restroom, go into a stall, and cry like a baby.

People, all of this could have been avoided. I did not have to move. I had a good job, my own apartment, my own car, and my own bank account. I was doing ok. I just put the cart before horse. I just did not take time and think, I made a big mistake. People, wake up! Don't do this to yourself. When someone wants you to move in with them, and keeps insisting on it by telling you how great it will be, don't go for it. It will eventually explode in your face, so beware. When I finished seeing the doctor, my children and I headed back to our apartment, and we stopped by my old apartment that I had turned over to my longtime childhood friend six months earlier. When Sandra let us into the apartment, she saw my condition and asked me what happened. I told her Justin had beaten me. She said, "I am very sorry to hear this, but I was just getting ready to leave. I will have to call you when I get back" as she politely walked us to the door.

Can you imagine how I felt, practically being asked to leave a place that was once my own?

People, people, don't be stupid! If you have a place of your own, you better hold on to it because there is an old cliché that goes like this, "God bless the child that has his own." Once we got back home, the gossip, the tension, and the talk in the neighborhood was so thick that you could cut through it with a knife. There was some talk around the neighborhood that Sandra was telling the neighbors that she didn't know why I came by her apartment, that I could not go back there, that it was her place now, and she was not about to give it up. The apartment was in her name, and that's the way it was going to stay.

The following Monday, I went and had a talk with my apartment manager, and she had to tell me she told me so. But Mrs. Jenkins was such a nice lady that she rented my little children and me another apartment the same day. She said, "Geraldine, I am mainly doing this for these little children so they won't get hurt. Geraldine, I am doing it for you as well. Don't be naive. Please don't do this again."

Mrs. Jenkins gave me the keys right there on the spot to a new apartment. The names in this book have been changed to protect the innocent, but Mrs. Jenkins, if you read this book, you will know who you are. And I must say I thank you and I do love you up until today. Thank you again.

Then I went on my way to find a moving company. On my way out of the apartment where the manager's office was, I passed Mr. T. standing on the back steps, looking up at the sky as usual, minding his own business. As we passed Mr. T., he said, "Just give me a name. I will take care of it for you."

He smiled and I smiled, and he asked, "Are you okay?"

I told him I was, and the children and I walked on back to Justin's apartment where we started packing and getting ready to move into our new place. We stayed there a little while, and then we went to see our new apartment. When we saw the new place, it was so nice that we just fell in the middle of the floor and started rolling around, laughing very loud and heartedly. We were so happy to finally have our own place once again. By the time Justin got out of jail, we had moved into our new apartment, three apartment buildings down.

I should have learned my lesson from that devastating situation, but I did not. I got involved with Mr. T., who was living about five buildings down from me with another woman.

What was happening to me was a mental condition that had taken over my life. I was no longer in control of my life. I was making the same mistakes over and over again, thinking things would turn out differently when they only got worse. I did not talk to Sandra for a very long time after that morning we visited her after leaving the hospital; I put that part of my life behind me and moved on.

Chapter 4

Be Careful of Whom You Call Your Friend

I began to let Mr. T. come by my new apartment to see me, and after a few months, I began to feel very close to Mr. T. I began to like him a lot. He was very attentive. However, my main focus was that I wanted Mr. Jam back and to make him my man again.

One night, I took a chance and went to Mr. Jam's home, the same home where I had taken the credit card back to. I walked up the stairs, and there was old girl, the one who was outside of Mr. Jam's home that rainy night throwing rocks up against the window, talking about how she knew what color sheets were on the bed.

Now it was too late for Mr. Jam and me. The lady had finally made it inside and redecorated the whole place. I had lost my best friend and lover because of my stupidity. I walked away because there was nothing else left for me to do; it was over. If I had known what I know now, that is where I would have left her—outside, throwing rocks—and continued on with my romance inside and let that drummer queen stay right where she was, outside. I should have not confronted

Mr. Jam about her behavior outside his window. The way I would handle that situation today is, I would have put my arms around him, pulled him close to me, and whispered in his ear, "Sweetheart, please promise me that you will not allow this to happen again." Following that statement, I would have turned over and went to sleep. That is the way I would have handled that matter today. But today, I am fifty-seven years old, and I sometimes ask myself why did I waste all of my young life being stupid?

People, people, wake up! Don't be stupid like I was. If you are involved with someone that cares about you so much that whatever your little heart desires, they make it available to you; and if there is any way you can stay with that person, care for them without hurting them, then it would be in everyone's best interest for you to do just that. Today, I would rather have been an old man's sweetheart than to be a young man's fool.

I had become one of those needy people, the kind who needs lots of so-called friends around. Yes, I said so-called because a true friend is very seldom found. A friend is like a jewel, very precious and very rare. So if by chance you find one, you hold on to them because a real, true friend very seldom comes along. I continued to hang out with the rat pack. You might say I am a little bitter, and yes, you would be right. But I will get over that as well.

During that time, I was between friends. I really didn't have any identity; I really did not know who I was and what I was capable of doing. As I look back on my life today, I realize I had so much potential, but I was not aware of it at that time. I always felt I needed to be validated by someone because I did not know how to validate myself. So I say to you people today, please know your self-worth, don't be taken advantage of, don't allow people to direct your path. Know who you are and what you want in life; once you do that, no one will be able to misuse you. So I started back having a lot of company again. One night, I was with two women that I thought were some very good friends of mine—guttersnippers, in reality.

So one evening, these two other females, or so-called friends, and I were sitting around my place and not doing anything special. I mentioned I had this friend, Thaddeus, who was a guy who liked to fish, and he had this large deep freezer with all types of fish in it, so I asked the ladies if they would like to go by his house and have some drinks, listen to some music, and eat some fish. That was something that Thaddeus did often. He had a great music library, so I thought that would be a good thing to do with my friends. They said, "Okay, that sounds like a winner." So I got on the telephone, called Thaddeus, and asked him if my two friends and I could come over. I told him I had two girlfriends that would like to come over and party for a little while. Thaddeus said that sounded good because he had a couple of his friends over as well, and we could come on over. So we got in my car and drove over to Thaddeus's home.

When we got there, both ladies were looking around in amazement and commenting about how nice a place he had and how beautifully decorated it was. I was tempted to tell them to sit down and chill out, but I did not.

So as the evening moved forward, the drinks got low, and Thaddeus said he would go to the store and pick up some more drinks. I had some marijuana in my purse; I wanted to smoke some weed, and I did not want to share it. I volunteered to go to the store by myself and pick up the drinks so I could make a stop on my way back and take a few hits off a joint before I returned to Thaddeus's home. Upon my return, I noticed a slight difference in everyone's attitude, but I did not let it bother me. I just blended right in and continued to party. After all, I had just smoked some weed, so I did not have a care in the world, not realizing that those couple of pulls off that joint was a part of my behavior that was going to eventually destroy my life.

When I was on the telephone earlier that afternoon, Thaddeus had mentioned that he was going fishing and asked me if I wanted to go with him. He said he and a couple of his friends were going up to the lake, renting a cabin, and staying for the weekend. I told him no because I had to be at work Saturday, but if I did not have to work, I would have been happy to go. I did not know what a problem this fishing trip would cause later on. So one of the ladies that was with me her name was Jasmine, she was my roommate. She had lost her apartment a few months earlier for none payment of rent. The other lady was Sabrina; it was at Sabrina's house where I took my first hit of crack cocaine. Sabrina's baby daddy was at her apartment on the evening that I am speaking of. His name was Quincy. Quincy was a worldly man who had access to many things, so they were looking for new recruits like myself. One evening, I was at my home resting after work; I had made dinner, fed my children, and put them to bed, minding my own business. There was a knock on my door; it was Sabrina, asking me if I wanted to come over to her apartment for a little while because she had something very interesting to show me. That should have been a warning right then. What could be interesting in a full-fledged drug addict's house other than more drugs? So being the out-of-control follower I had become, I told her to give me a few minutes, and I would be right over.

A few minutes later, I went over to Sabrina's house, and that is where I saw this strange monstrosity sitting on her dining room table. It was shaped or in the form of a large, long clear-glass snake. It was a large crack pipe, something I had never seen before in my life. But that is how so many addicts get themselves into so much trouble, having that addictive personality, being curious, wanting to know what makes things click, and all that dumb stuff. When I saw that glass monstrosity sitting on Sabrina's dining room table, I sat down, and I wanted to know what function that monstrosity had. Quincy asked, "Would you like to try this?" Not knowing what I was saying yes to, I told him "Yes." If I had known like I know now, I would have turned around and ran like hell. Quincy put three large twenty-dollar cocaine rocks on the screen of that glass pipe and told me to pull on it as hard as I could as he held the torch to it, and I did, and that was the beginning of a sixteen year crack cocaine addiction.

People, people, don't be stupid! If it looks like a snake, is shaped like a snake, and has snake eyes, people, please listen. It *is* a snake! Please don't get yourself involved in something that can and will hurt you just because you are curious, because it can be deadly. I just told you this to let you know how one act that I did without thinking had ruined my life; that evening was the beginning of many years of my crack cocaine addiction.

Now back to the fishing trip with Thaddeus. One of the two ladies that I took over to Thaddeus's home was living with me at the time; her name was Jasmine. As I told you earlier in the book, Jasmine had been evicted. So I allowed her to move in with me, which was a temporary move. It was only to be until she got back on her feet and found a new place to live. I went along with that because we were supposed to have been a tight-knit group, very close friends, or so I thought.

So we enjoyed the evening and had a great time. After everyone got good and drunk, I decided it was time to leave, knowing I had to go to work the following morning. Realizing there was not a sober driver in the house, I drove home despite of that. After arriving home, Sabrina went home, and Jasmine and I went to my apartment. Jasmine went to her room, and I went to my room and retired for the night. The following morning, I got up, took my bath, got dressed, and went to work, leaving Jasmine asleep at my home. I worked all that Saturday thinking about how well things had gone at Thaddeus's home on Friday night. On that following Monday morning, Thaddeus called me and asked if he could come over. He said he had something to talk to me about that was very important, and that my life could possibly depend on it. With Thaddeus being so sure that my life could depend upon this visit, I was very concerned about what he really had to tell me. So I quickly told Thaddeus to come on over.

Thaddeus arrived at my home about thirty minutes later; he was very excited and anxious.

I said, "Calm down before you start telling me why you feel my life could be in danger because now I am worried about you." I got him calmed down, and he then began to tell me what happened. Thaddeus told me he had called my home last Saturday morning to see if I would reconsider and go on the fishing trip with him.

I said, "Well, that is okay. Thaddeus, you are still all right with me." And I just laughed it off.

Thaddeus said, "No, Geraldine, you don't understand. That is not all that happened. Brace yourself. Please don't be angry with me." I said, "Come on, stop playing around. Angry at you for what?" Thaddeus said, "When I called Saturday morning, Jasmine answered your telephone, and I asked her had you left for work yet, and Jasmine told me yes, that you had already left for work." I told him I had left early Saturday morning because we had an early morning employees meeting.

Thaddeus said, "Well, what happened is this. Jasmine then asked, 'Would you like to leave a message?' I told her, 'No, I was only going to ask her if I could change her mind about going fishing with me instead of going to work, and I would take care of all her expenses including work.' Jasmine said that didn't seem like a problem to her. Not only would she go fishing with me, but her friend Sabrina from next door would go as well and entertain me and my friend, Dennis. And without thinking, I told her okay. Jasmine then said, 'You don't have to pick us up because we know how to get over to your house.' I said, 'Okay, come on. Get here soon because Dennis and I will be leaving in about an hour.' Jasmine said, 'Okay.'"

I was surprised and asked if they showed up. He told me that not only did they show up, the two of them went on the fishing trip with him. I said, "No shit?"

Thaddeus said, "No shit."

Jasmine was occupying my son's room, where she was at the time Thaddeus was telling me about their trip to the lake together.

So I said, "Jasmine, come out here. Thaddeus was telling me that you and Sabrina went on the fishing trip with him and Dennis. Is this true?"

Jasmine said, "Wait a minute, Geraldine. Let me explain what happened."

Thaddeus said, "There is nothing to explain. You and Sabrina went on the fishing trip with Dennis and me. You slept in the bed with me, we had sex, and after sex, I kicked you out of my bed onto the floor, and I called you a dirty b. I asked you how could you be so dirty to someone who is as nice to you as Geraldine, and I also told you that as soon as I could speak with Geraldine, I was going to come clean and tell her what happened. And you begged me not to do so, and here I am telling her anyway. There you go, Geraldine. I was afraid of the harm that Jasmine could have done to you if I hadn't told you about the trip that we went on together, due to the fact that she lives in your home. Please don't hate me. I would rather you hate me than for Jasmine to have the opportunity to hurt you. I hope we can work through this, Geraldine."

I asked Jasmine, "Is this true?" Jasmine told me, "Yes."

I said, "Jasmine, after all I have done for you, for you to go behind my back and sneak off and go on a trip with a person that I consider more than a friend, who I was nice enough to introduce you to as my roommate and friend … I treated you like a sister, and you turn around and stab me in my back like this?"

Jasmine told me, "I am sorry, Geraldine. I should not have done that."

I said, "Never mind, Jasmine. Just go and pack your things, and you and Thaddeus both get the hell out of my home, and I mean like yesterday!"

When they left, I went into my bedroom, lay down across my bed, and thought about what part I played in that whole situation.

People, people, don't be stupid! If you have someone who you are interested in to the point that you would like them as your partner, you don't need to take people to their home to drink and get drunk because you are asking for trouble. I know you might say if you can't trust them, well, you don't need them. But you must remember one should examine the character of a person before you let them get close to you or your loved ones because drug addicts cannot be trusted. I don't care who they are. This makes me think of the story of the old lady who found an injured alligator lying by the side of a riverbank. The old lady wrapped that alligator up in her apron, took it home with her, nursed it back to health, and fed it until it was fat and healthy. You know what that alligator did? The alligator ate her alive. The old lady was far down in the alligator's belly, and the old lady said, "I wrapped you in my apron, brought you home with me, nursed you back to health, and I fed you until you got fat. Now you turn around and eat me alive. How could you do this to me?"

The alligator said, "You knew what I did for a living when you took me in. I eat people alive. What did you expect?" That is what an out-of-control drug addict will do to you as well; no matter how nice you are to one of them, if they catch you slipping, the drug addict will eat you alive and never look back. So, people, take a thorough inventory of whom you deal with in this life because a real drug addict doesn't give a damn about crossing you.

So life went on, and I continued to work and get high. I also got more involved with Mr. T. He was eye candy at that time; nice to look at and sweet to the touch. We started being together fairly often. After about six months of steady intimacy, I got pregnant by Mr.

T. I was very happy about the pregnancy. A pregnancy that wasn't planned, but a pregnancy that I wanted. I was okay with it. I was so in love with Mr. T.; he was everything I wanted in a man, and I was extremely happy.

At that time, I did not have any family here in Los Angeles to talk to about how I felt about Mr. T. Have you ever had some good news and no one to tell it to? I was bursting to tell someone my good news; I couldn't keep it to myself. That was the way I felt on the morning the doctor told me I was pregnant. I knew the baby belonged to Mr. T. because I was not sexually active with anyone but Mr. T.

I had some concerns about my relationship with Mr. T. and no one to talk to. My main concern was my two children. What would they think? I had already taken them through enough; I thought to myself, *When will this all end?* And you must remember, I did not have a good education at the time. With all my education combined, I had, at the most, an eleventh grade education. So there was a lot about life that I really did not understand. I had some street knowledge, but not a lot of book knowledge. Whether you know it or not, that will create a great void in your life.

One evening, I was sitting at home all alone, no one to talk to, and who stopped by my home? None other than Jasmine! I asked her what was the purpose of her stopping by my home, and she said she had been thinking of me a lot. Jasmine dropped by on that happy, lonely, and mixed emotions-filled day, and I began to tell her my good news about the pregnancy. She immediately said, "Are you sure you want to go through with this?" Never saying, "How do you feel about it?" or "Do you think this is something that you can endure?" I should have recognized the negativity at that moment, but I was too involved in the fact that I was carrying Mr. T's baby; I was not thinking clearly. If I had been in my right mind, I would have sent Jasmine on her way.

People, people, wake up! You know when someone has your best interest at heart and when he or she doesn't. Don't be stupid; know who you are involved with. If you have more negative memories of a person than positive ones, then you know that person does not have your best interest at heart. Don't be stupid, people, wake up and smell the coffee before it turns into tea. Being so anxious to tell someone about my good news that I had been keeping to myself for about a month, I let the negativity coming from Jasmine slide right by me instead of checking her right at that moment. That's another big mistake I made.

Jasmine and I would have the conversation about Mr. T. and my plans practically daily. She would never tell me anything good or helpful concerning my unborn child, whom I was already in love with although still in my belly. By this time, Jasmine had moved back into my home. I allowed myself to be manipulated by her cunning ways. Jasmine was about ten years older than I was and had been on the streets much longer than I had.

It was about three months later when I became disappointed with Mr. T. because Jasmine had put into my head that if Mr. T. wanted me, my family, and the little unborn baby, he would move from where he was staying and move in with me. How cunning of her!

So one evening, Mr. T. and I were spending a romantic evening together, and I got so involved until I could not hold back on telling Mr. T. that I wanted him. I said, "Baby, if you really love me the way you say you do, you would move in with me tonight."

Mr. T. said, "Baby, I love you with everything I have, but please don't ask me to make that move tonight. I am not quite ready right now. I am going to make that move. But, baby, please don't ask me to do that tonight. It would not be fair to me, to you, and to all that are involved."

We continued to drink and talk, and the more I drank, the drunker I got—and more needy—to the point that I begged Mr. T. to move in with us. I continued to ask him to move in with me until he just gave up and said, "Okay, Geraldine, but whatever happens, please don't let anything happen to our baby because if you do, you will never forgive yourself because not only are you a good mother and a good woman, we are in love."

The last thing I remember about that night is, I fell asleep lying in his lap, and I left my door unlocked, waiting for him to return with his clothes and move in, which he never did. What woke me up a few hours after Mr. T. had left was Jasmine coming in my door. I was still drunk and out of control, and did not have a clue about what was about to happen to me, something that would turn my life upsidedown.

Jasmine and I sat there on my sofa, and I told her how Mr. T. had lied to me about coming back with his clothes and moving in with me. Jasmine said, "Girl, that is a damn shame. He did not have to lie to you like that, girl."

I was still out of it. I could not read between the lines about what she was saying, and I was so blind that I could not see.

I said, "I don't know if I should have this baby or not."

That was all Jasmine needed to hear. She said, "Now that you are thinking straight, this is something you need to seriously think about." I started thinking, and all kinds of negative things started to pop into my head.

I was at the doctor's office about a month earlier, and he was telling me if I wasn't sure about having my baby that there were options that were open to me, and he gave me some addresses, names, and some numbers. I took them and returned home and put them away without considering using them. I told Jasmine that if I wasn't so drunk, I would go and see if I could find one of those abortion clinics that my doctor had given me the address to and end all of this because Mr. T. did not have to lie to me. I was having a pity party, which was when Jasmine spoke up and told me that "Just because you have been drinking, that is not a problem. I will drive you." I told her I didn't know what the doctors would think about the fact that I had been drinking all night. Jasmine said, "That is not a problem either. Situations like yours happen all the time."

I finally made up my mind and said, "Okay." I got myself somewhat together, and we went out to my car. She sat in the driver's seat; I got on the backseat with my head hanging out of the window just in case I had to throw up.

My children were down at the babysitter's house. I am going to call her Sweet Sadie. Sweet Sadie would often talk to me about the people that I was hanging around with.

She would say, "Geraldine, you need to keep those people out of your house. Those people you are hanging around are nothing but trouble. They don't mean you any good. Please listen to me before it is too late."

I told Sweet Sadie I was going to listen to her.

She said, "Okay now, I am going to hold you to this, Sweetie Pie." That is what she used to call me.

So Jasmine and I were driving on out of the back gate, and on our way out of the driveway, one of my other neighbors was standing out on her back steps. Her name was Sandy, may God rest her soul. Sandy said, "Hey, wait a minute, where are you all headed to?"

Jasmine said, "I am about to take Geraldine to take care of some business. We will be right back."

Sandy replied, "Geraldine, are you sure you want to go and take care of this business now? Can't it wait until later?" Sandy knew something wasn't right.

I said, "No, I will go and take care of it now." Mrs. Sandy said, "Well, okay then."

So Jasmine and I drove to the abortion clinics, to the first address that I had supplied her with. When we got to the first clinic, there were people picketing, but instead of going back home, Jasmine suggested to try the other address where there might not be anyone picketing. I agreed, and we proceeded to the other abortion clinic that I had the address to and had given to Jasmine. Jasmine was driving and talking just as if we were on our way to a picnic, no problem at all. I knew what

I was about to do was wrong; I felt it deep down in my soul. We arrived at the other address that we had for the abortion clinics. It was quiet; no one was boycotting, clear sailing. We walked right in and right up to the receptionist window, and Jasmine said, "Geraldine is here for an abortion."

The lady said, "Have a seat. Someone will be with you very shortly."

I started to fill out the paperwork, and Jasmine finished it for me and gave it to me to sign. A few minutes later, the nurse came and took me to the abortion room—a room I will never forget. The first thing they told me was to get undressed, put this gown on, and get on the table. I did. Right after I got on the table, the nurse gave me an injection—anesthesia, I later found out.

I don't remember much after that except realizing and knowing that this was something that I did not want to go through with. I was waving my hands telling the lady that I didn't want to do this. "Please stop, and let me up." All I can remember is hearing voices saying, "It is too late now. We cannot turn back. We are too far into the process." After that, it seemed as if I was on a roller coaster going around really fast. All I could see was Sweet Sadie's big, beautiful round face, and she was saying, "See, Geraldine, I told you to leave those no good people alone. See, if you had listened to me, we would not be here now." All I could do was cry like a baby. People, people, please listen to me! I destroyed a life and a relationship that could have lasted forever. That is how strong my love was for that child and for Mr.T.

People, people, wake up! Don't be stupid. I would give anything to be able to turn that horrible act around and bring that child on into this world. I would not wish this on anyone; there is not a day that goes by I don't regret what I did on that foggy day. After the abortion was completed, Jasmine and I drove back home, and instead of Jasmine coming in to my home, she walked in, gave me my keys, and got some things that belonged to her then went downstairs with the rest of the rat pack for the rest of the evening. She knew what we had done was wrong, but I was more at fault than she was. I came in laid down and went to sleep.

I was awakened by a phone call. Mr. T. was on the phone, and the very first thing that came out of his mouth was something I will never forget.

He said, "Geraldine, baby, what have you done?"

I froze. I actually could not move. That was the first time that I had been sober in twenty-four hours. I said, "Baby, wait a minute, let me explain."

Mr. T. said, "Explain what? Please don't tell me nothin' stupid." I told him to come over because I needed to talk to him. Mr. T. came right over, and the first thing he asked me was 'How is our baby doing?' and the first thing I did was lie.

I said, "Well, you know, that is what I wanted to talk to you about. The doctor made a mistake. There was never a baby. I was not pregnant."

Mr. T. said, "Stop that lie right now. Until you are able to find our misplaced baby, the one you say never existed, don't speak to me. Do you understand me, Ms. Thomas?"

I had never heard him call me by my last name the entire time I had known him. I knew then I had screwed up. For the first time in my life, I had found true love, and I had the nerve to do what I did and go out like a real sucker.

It took me approximately six years to be able to sleep through the night. And right now, to this day, I still have restless nights about that day in the abortion clinic. And today, I don't know the street or the addresses of either one of those clinics that I went to on that heartbreaking day. I could not tell you where those clinics were located if you paid me. That is how badly I wanted to erase that memory from my mind. I do believe if I had not been involved with drugs, alcohol, and people like Jasmine, I would have my baby today.

People, people, wake up! Don't be stupid. If you have a person in your life that is willing to drive you someplace to kill one of your children that they have never seen before in their life, then there is no limit to the harm they will do to you. Come on now, breathe in through your nose and out through your mouth. I do believe after all the mistakes I have made in my lifetime, one should think before they act. Look at the big picture because there are consequences that are involved with every decision you make.

I remember reaching for Mr. T. to put my arms around him, but he backed up with both hands in the air, walking backward and saying, "Please don't touch me! Don't you put your hands on me until you can give me my baby back!" That is when I said, "Baby, please, we can make another one."

In the lowest tone that I have ever heard him speak in, Mr. T. said, "What do you mean make another one? I wanted that baby. You can't replace babies like you would replace a pair of shoes, Geraldine. What the hell is wrong with you? When my baby comes back, that is when I'll come back. Good-bye."

When Mr. T. walked out of my door and closed it, I fell to the floor crying uncontrollably, and I stayed there for hours and hours, just rolling around on the floor. I cried myself to sleep, holding my stomach, knowing that my baby was not coming back.

Early that next morning, I finally gained enough strength to get up and go the kitchen and get a drink of water. I can remember it was the worst tasting water I had ever tasted in my life. Sometimes I wonder if it was the bitter taste of the water or the taste that Mr. T. had left in my mouth.

I knew I had to start getting myself together because it would not be long before my children would be coming home from Sweet Sadie's house, and I had to be somewhat composed before they got in. I used to think that Mr. T. knew about my abortion just because he felt it, but later I found out that some of those rat pack guttersnippers told him about it. Let me tell you, I also found out later that Jasmine had told Mr. T. she would give anything for him to make love to her for just one night. I did not find this out until later, after I had destroyed three lives with one act.

People, people, please, listen! Some of us are always talking about how someone has taken our mate, but most of the time, we are the ones who have given them away. How? By advertising to our friends how nice our partners are, how good they make us feel, how faithful they are, how caring they are, how delicately they hold us, how much financial support they give us, what nice restaurants they take us to, the five-star hotels we vacation at, etc. Because the setup is so sweet, you have received some good news, and you have to tell somebody about it. Sometimes we need to keep that to ourselves. Certain things your partner does for you, and with you, need to be kept sacred; hold it near and dear to your heart. Have you ever heard a person say, "He sure is good to her. I wish I had someone that would treat me like that." People, people, wake up! Don't be stupid. They are not lying, and they will do anything in their power to make it happen. If you think I am lying to you, keep it up; and if it has not happened to you yet, stop advertising because that is all you are doing when you keep doing those things that I just quoted. The truth is, they want what you auction off.

No one knows what you have in your pocket until you tell them. Some things are meant for you to know and for others to never find out.

Like Mr. T. said, "You can go to the store and buy a pair of shoes and go home with them. If you don't like them once you try them on, you can take them back to the store with your receipt and get your refund back. But with an abortion, once you go and make that transaction, there is no refund. You got nothing coming. It is over for good." So before you go there, make sure you can live with the consequences. Please, believe me, there will be consequences.

Jasmine moved out of my home after that abortion without me telling her to move. That is why, today, I feel it was a setup, and I helped her carry it out.

Today, my child would be thirty-two years old, and there has not been a day gone by that I haven't thought about that baby. People, don't make your move too soon without thinking about the consequences. This is the first time I am speaking about that day in that abortion clinic to anyone. The reason I am speaking about it today is because I feel that the child should have lived, should have been given a chance to grow up and be all God meant him to be. I say *him* because in my heart, I believe he was a male child. No one ever told me that the baby was a boy; this is just a strong feeling I have deep down in my soul.

Another thing I know today is that God is not going to give you a child that you cannot take care of. I wish I had given birth to that child, even if I had to put him up for adoption; at least there might be a chance for us to come together. But when you resort to abortion, there will never be a chance of that happening. Now this is just my truth no one else.

Mr. T., if you are out there, I pray to God that you will find it in your heart to forgive me, if you haven't already, because I am truly sorry. I would give anything to be able to turn that act around and be given the opportunity to have you sit by my side in a delivery room and have you witness the birth of our child. May God bless you, Mr. T., wherever you are. For what it is worth, I still love you. And first of all, I pray that God will forgive me for all the sins I have committed.

Chapter 5

❦

A Dope Fiend Move

I continued to live in that same apartment complex. You would think by now that I would have learned my lesson. But you will read how some people like me could not easily shake drugs and alcohol and those old dope fiend moves that are often made by drug addicts and alcoholics. For example, stupidity and insanity come with using drugs and alcohol. There is nothing good about being a drug addict or an alcoholic. So if you are not involved with that scene, don't get involved because there is no winning in it.

There was this female (we will call this female Samantha) who lived in the building where I lived. She started to come around, visiting my home, pretending to be my friend, telling me she heard about what happened with Mr. T. and me, and telling me about how sorry she was about what I had gone through. Again, here I was trusting and being a needy person again. Samantha lived down the hall from me. She would always come down to my place to watch TV. I should have known something was funny about her due tothe fact that she would always come to my home asking for things that she already had at her own home. I should have smelled a rat. Plus, she always asked me to give her something to cook for her children from my refrigerator. Samantha was working, and I was too. As a matter of fact, I think she was making a little bit more money than I was. Because I was born and raised in Mississippi, I still had that old southern hospitality mind-set. You know, if someone is hungry, you feed him or her. End of story, no question asked. Samantha began to stick to me like glue; everywhere I turned, she was right there. The drug and alcohol scene continued to go on in my apartment; Samantha was another slick guttersnipper. She wasn't a really serious drug addict. She just watched everything everyone else was doing so she could get things going her way and to be able to report the situation just like it happened. Plus, she would add to it as well. That was another thing that I was not aware of at the time.

I had to be a mighty stupid person to be used that much by that many people. Today, when I think about my life, I realize I am blessed to still be alive after all the bad things I allowed to happen to me. I don't care what type of drug addict or alcoholic you are; your Higher Power will heal you just by asking. The reason why I know this is because he healed me, and I was a drug addict in the worst way. You know, there is an old saying that goes like this, "He may not come exactly when you want him to, but he always comes on time." I am a living witness, and I choose to call my Higher Power my Lord and Savior, Jesus Christ. You may call yours whatever you want to. Just call; it will work for you. I believe it will. But who am I?

Samantha was ordering food from my house so regularly at one time that I felt she was grocery shopping out of my kitchen. Samantha was a shrewd operator; she would come to my apartment and say to me, "Geraldine, you sure are a nice person. I am glad we are friends."

And I would tell her that I was glad we were friends as well.

Here I go being stupid again, and I did not know it.

At one time I had come into a nice amount of money. I gave my children about a thousand dollars and let them go to Sweet Sadie's home for a few days, and the party at my place began for one solid month straight. All I can remember is that I was constantly buying drugs—morning, noon, and night. Around that third week of drug using and partying, a lot of my "friends" started thinning out. They began to realize that my money was about to run out, and they did not want me to come knocking on their door after it was all gone. I was buying drugs for couples, man and wife, man and girlfriend, man and man, girl and girl—whoever came in the house. Everything was on me, and they partied like rock stars.

However, when that fourth week came around, I looked in my purse and saw what was left of all that money. I had no other choice but to hit the floor one more time. I was screaming, hollering so loud. One could hear me at least five blocks away. That was how hurt I was. That big crowd that was hanging around me had vanished. How stupid can one person be?

People, people, wake up and stop being stupid. Most people don't care about you; they care about what they can get out of you. I learned that when your money is gone, most of the time, your friends are gone also, especially the type of friends I had at that time. With friends like those, you don't need any enemies.

People, people, wake up! Stop being stupid! If you have a chance to get some money where you will have enough to make someone happy, please start within your home, with your family, with people that love you, so when your money is gone, they will still be there. The people in the street are just what I said; they are people in the street. They will not be there when the chips are down. Trust me, I know.

Things got really bad after I discovered I had very little money left and fewer friends; they both were gone. I received an eviction notice to vacate my apartment. That was really, really disturbing news to me because I had no family in Los Angeles to help me or to fall back on. So I was just stuck.

What happened with the eviction was that I was taken to court, and I won. So I was ordered to pay my back rent, and I did. I did not have a problem with that. I paid my back rent and had good intentions to move forward with my life. However, the assistant manager of the apartment complex had other plans in mind for me.

After accepting my back rent, he came up with this wild idea that I owed court cost. I argued that fact, but the assistant manager insisted that I did indeed owe court cost. The assistant manager and Samantha were close friends, which I did not know at that time. I would often wonder why, after all the years that I had lived in that apartment complex without any problem, and all of a sudden, I ended up in court. I did not understand where all the hostility from the manager's office was coming from. There is an old saying that goes like this, "What goes on in the dark will soon come to light" and "What goes into the wash will defiantly come out in the rinse." Those are some true quotes, I truly believe.

Samantha would show up at my door whenever she would hear someone come to my home or whenever she would hear any type of music coming from my home. Prior to all my troubles I went out and purchased a new car, two weeks later, Samantha went out and bought a new car also. As often as she would borrow things from me, one would think that she would not be able to purchase anything, much less a new car. But she did. I should have recognized the pattern of how she was always on my heels. That should have told me something right there. But being such a needy drug addict and alcoholic, I could not see the forest for the trees. I was totally blind to everything that was going on around me if it did not involve drugs and alcohol. If I did not think this book would help someone, it would be much harder for me to write it or it wouldn't get written at all because it brings back so many bad memories. People, people, wake up! Stop being stupid, and smell the coffee before it turns into tea. People, listen to me. If you are involved with someone, I don't care who they are, male or female, who is always coming to you with their hands out, begging for any and everything that you have, and never once comes to you and says something to this effect, "Well, I know this is not much to offer compared to what you have done and do for me, I just feel it is no more than right for me to come with something just to show you my appreciation. But when my ship comes in, I will do better."

Now that is something you can understand. But if you got someone always knocking on your door asking for something and never bringing anything in, it is time to evaluate this because something about that is just not right. It is time to cut your ties because you are losing, and there is no opportunity for you to gain anything.

Samantha would never run out of gas for her car, her utilities were never turned off, and she always dressed nicely. It was just things she needed for her house and her family that she was always knocking on my door for, and I was always on the giving end, never the receiving. That doesn't add up to anything; it makes you a bigger loser than you already are.

Samantha was the mother of six children, and at that time, I was the mother of two children. In the complex I lived in, I was in one of the largest apartments there, and it was very nice, if I must say so. I also found out later that Samantha was the next one on the list in the manager's office to get the next large apartment when the next one became available. I didn't know this at that time.

Let me tell you a little something about Gwendolyn. Gwendolyn was the slick guttersnipper that pretended to be so naive, but all the time, she was getting over on people. I got involved with some new people, and there was this one lady that I had been hanging around with. She was married to this young man who lived in the building next to me. She lived with her husband and his mother. She was one of those drug users that only used when someone else was buying. I used to think that it was because she could not afford it, but later I found out that was a lie as well. We are going to call her Gwendolyn. Gwendolyn was one of those southern chicks that knew how to be slick, and you would never recognize it because she covered her slickness up by playing naive.

At the time, I was working the swing shift and had a bar in my apartment that was fully equipped with mostly anything you wanted to drink. Every night, I would get off work and there would be this whole group of people waiting on me, ready to go to my apartment to drink, eat, and listen to my music all night long for free. How stupid could I be?

People don't use you because they are smarter than you are. People will only use you if you allow them to. Remember that. Today, I realize I don't have very much, but what I do have is needed by my children, myself, my grandchildren, and my great grandchildren. They can use everything I have to offer. There are some things that you just cannot buy. For example, love, friends, and happiness. These are just a few of the things that you cannot buy. A price tag is not on some things. If it is not for you, then it is just not for you; I don't care how much you pay. So you might as well wake up and smell the coffee before it turns into tea.

Now back to Gwendolyn. One evening, the whole gang was at my home one more time. Gwendolyn proclaimed she was pregnant by one of the neighbors that she tricked into marrying her. We were all at my home when all of a sudden, she pretended to get really sick due to her pregnancy and asked if she could go lie down in my bed until she felt better. I had just recently redecorated my bedroom. I had this very expensive comforter on my bed with matching drapes, throw pillows, shams, wall plaque, all matching; it was really nice. I had just finished showing off my newly decorated bedroom to all the ladies in the house. So I let her lie down across my bed, and I asked if there was anything else I could do to make her feel better.

She said, "No, I will be fine if I lay down for a few minutes." I left her there and went back into the living room where everybody was partying.

Approximately one hour later, I heard all of this noise coming from my bedroom. So I rushed in there, and there was Gwendolyn lying in a puddle of vomit on my bed.

I said, "What in the hell have you done in my bed? You couldn't make it to the damn bathroom? Have you lost your f—— mind? What in the hell is wrong with you? Get your ass out of my bed!"

She replied, "I am so sorry, Geraldine, but I was so sick. I just could not make it to the bathroom. Please forgive me." This was some more of that slick stuff that I was telling you about earlier. I told the others the party was over and told Ben to come and get his wife because I had to make a run to the dry cleaner's right away.

They all left. I gathered my comforter up, put it in a large green plastic bag, went out, got into my car, and rushed it to the dry cleaner's. I was pissed off all the way there. I knew it was done on purpose because my bathroom was right down the hall from my bedroom. Gwendolyn could have crawled there if necessary to keep from vomiting in my bed.

People, people, wake up! Listen to me! When you are involved with someone that is always messing up and destroying your property, it is time for you to cut all ties with that person because it is not going to get any better. The longer you hang on, hoping this person will change, the greater your loss will be because you cannot teach an old goat a different way to chew. That person is not going to stop until they have destroyed everything you have. Please believe me. I am telling you what I know. You don't need jealous people around you, especially if you are trying to go somewhere in life to be successful. They will always be a hindrance to you, especially when you are involved with negative people like I was.

As soon as I made it back home from the dry cleaner's, here comes Samantha, rushing down the hallway. "Hi, Geraldine. May I have a cup of sugar?"

I wanted to say, "Bitch, when are you going to start buying groceries?" I was about tired of her now; my bedspread had just got messed up, and now here she was, begging as usual. And then Samantha had the nerve to say, "Geraldine, I heard something happened down here involving Gwendolyn. What happened?"

I said, "Nothing happened here. Why do you ask?"

She said, "Oh, never mind. I just thought something happened. Okay then, I will see you later, Geraldine. Oh, yeah, thank you!" So that just goes to show you that when you have a microscope on you where you live, any and everything that goes on in your home, the whole world will know about it as soon as it happens. This may sound harsh, but the fewer people who know about you and your business, the better off you are.

The news about the comforter had spread quickly. That is the way people are, especially the type of people I was dealing with. I am not saying everyone is like that. Don't get me wrong. I am speaking of what happened to me in the circle I was in. I am speaking my facts, which are all I can give in my writing. So I should have cut all ties with Gwendolyn right then, but I didn't. How stupid can one person be?

So one evening, Gwendolyn and I were downstairs in one of my new apartments that Mrs. Jenkins had rented to me one more time. The only things I moved into that newly decorated apartment were a stereo, albums, and drinking glasses. Oh yes, and of course, drug paraphernalia. For example, crack pipes, cotton balls, and a burner. Anything that had something to do with crack cocaine, I had it. Not only did I have those things for myself, I also had those things for my so-called friends as well.

People, let me tell you what happened on that very day. Gwendolyn and I were sitting in my master bedroom getting high, and I stepped away for a few minutes to get some ice from the refrigerator. Oh yes, I forgot to tell you that the apartment was so beautiful and fully equipped. It came with a brand-new stove and refrigerator. How sweet could it get? I was out of the master bedroom for just a few minutes. When I returned to my bedroom, all I could see was a large blaze coming from my beautiful, brand- new green carpet. I immediately started screaming, "Gwendolyn, what the hell is happening in here? What are you doing, b——? How can you do this to me, as nice as I am to you? How mean can you get? You should be ashamed of yourself!"

People, people, it is not that Gwendolyn should have been ashamed of herself; the real blame was on me. I should have been ashamed of myself. I had my priorities mixed up. I was the one who had the keys to my brand-new apartment.

The only way Gwendolyn could have gotten into my master bedroom with all that crack and fire was if I let her in. So the blame was on *me*. Like I said, people, wake up and stop being stupid. People don't use you because they are smarter than you. People only use you because you allow them to. That is a fact. I thank my Lord and Savior, Jesus Christ, for saving my life because he brought me a mighty long way. He saved my life. I had people tell me to my face that I was not going to live another year, but God saw it differently. God looked beyond my faults and saw my needs. That's why today I can write this book and not be ashamed because the scripture says, "If you are ashamed to acknowledge me before your friends, I will be ashamed to acknowledge you before my Father."

I believe my life was saved for this purpose—among others, to write this book, to get the word out there from a recovering alcoholic and drug addict like myself; to let the sick and suffering alcoholics and drug addicts know that you don't have to live your life running scared every day and every night, walking around with no place to go, everyone slamming their doors in your face; you knock and don't get any answers. That is no way to live your life. There is a God who will heal your mind and your body. He is just waiting on you to come to Him. Just for asking and being persistent, He will heal you. What are you waiting on? He is waiting on you. Please don't wait until it is too late. I say this because so many of my friends did not make it. And one more time, I told Gwendolyn, "You got to go. I can finish getting high by myself. After all, I bought everything alone.

Why not use it alone?"

Gwendolyn said okay and left. I sat there alone, and I felt like a stupid little fool. Another one of my mistakes was that although God had blessed me with this nice newly refurbished apartment, I had let her in. The only people that should have gone into that apartment with me were my two little children, and the Holy Book. I should have taken my babies into that apartment and asked God to bless us and our home. That would have been the right thing to do, but being the out-of-control drug addict that I was, I did everything but that. How stupid could I have been?

Let me say something to you. Our future of being successful in life depends on the choices we make. Please try to make good choices in life rather than bad ones. A lot of the time, we walk around saying "Poor me, poor me." That is not it. Most of the time, it is the choices we make in life that determines the path our life will take. Please, wake up and stop being stupid before the coffee turns into tea. Now breathe into your nose and out through your mouth.

Remember, I told you earlier that I had received an eviction notice to move for nonpayment of rent, which I had paid already, but that the assistant manager, Mr. B., felt I should have paid courtcost. Well, I was told by my peers that I was not liable for that, and I took their word for it. Do you know what that is called? That is called a *dope fiend move*, taking other people's advice without checking it out for yourself. Given the fact that you are a drug addict, and the people who are giving the advice are drug addicts as well, that is called a dope fiend move.

From my perspective, my truth—I told you in the beginning of this book that this book is based on my truth and my truth only, no one else's. If anyone can get anything out of this book, I would call it a blessing. It is not meant to be a cure. Don't stop taking your medicine. Don't stop anything you were doing before you started reading my book. This is my truth, and my truth is only for your reading pleasure.

So one day, my children were in the apartment when all of a sudden, one of my children came running to the apartment where I was smoking crack and said, "Mama, the people are at our house telling us we got five minutes to get our stuff and get out. Mama, please help!"

You could have bought me for a plug nickel. That was how cheap I felt. So I hesitantly got up from the table and went to my apartment.

There was Mr. B., the assistant manager, with some other people telling me I had to get all the belongings that I could get and be out of the apartment within five minutes. After living there for approximately ten years, that was a very devastating blow. I told Mr. B that I had accumulated ten years' worth of stuff, and could he please give me at least one more day to find somewhere to take my belongings to. He said to the people who were escorting him, "Will you allow me to take the lock, and I will come back here tomorrow and lock the door myself? Ms. Thomas deserves that much."

The people said it was okay. Mr. B, the assistant manager, took the lock and told me, "Ms. Thomas, you have until tomorrow evening at five o'clock to have your belongings out of this apartment, or I will lock you out and everything that is in here will be locked in. Do you understand me, Ms. Thomas?"

I told him yes. My heart was about to burst, but I could not allow Mr. B. to see that. I also had to be strong for my little children. I had messed up enough. I had no idea what I was going to do at that particular time.

But let me tell you about the God that I serve today. I may not be where I want to be in Christ today, but one thing I know for sure: I am not where I used to be. Let me share something with you: I was so devastated about what was happening to my family and me that all I could do was walk to the window outside in the hallway of my apartment and look out. I was looking with no directions in sight of where I was going to go, but let me tell you what happened. I was just standing there, too weak to fight when, out of the blue, one of my friends whom I hadn't seen in approximately eight years walked up. I looked down; I said to myself, "Is that who I think it is? No! There is no way that can be her!" I called out her name, "Dolly Dimple!"

She replied, "Yes, Ms. Cadillac, this is Dolly Dimple."

I asked her what she was doing over here. She said, "Looking for you, Ms. Cadillac."

Those were the names we had given each other approximately nine years prior to that evening. That is why I say that not everyone is a guttersnipper. This was a lady whom I called my friend fromthe day I met her. Even up to this day, I still call her my friend.

When I realized that it really was Dolly, I ran to her with both arms wide open. I must have held her for about three minutes before letting her go. I said, "You would not believe what is happening to me right now as we speak." I continued, "Dolly, I am being evicted from my home, and I have no place to take my furniture."

Dolly said, "Ms. Cadillac, this must be your lucky day, and let me tell you why. My roommate and I just rented an apartment in the Valley, and we do not have any furniture. So we would be happy to keep your furniture until you find yourself another place to live."

I told her that I did not have any way to get my furniture out to the Valley, and she said, "That is not a problem. I have a friend with a very large truck, and he will come and pick your furniture up and take it to our new apartment in the Valley at no charge. As soon as you find your new home, you can get your furniture back without delay, and I will take very good care of your furniture as well."

That was such a big relief for me that God had sent a real true friend to me in a time of need. Plus, He was so on time! So I know you are out there, Dolly. If you read this book, please contact me. I would love to hear from you.

Dolly left me that evening saying, "Geraldine, don't worry. I will see you early in the morning."

The very next morning, Dolly and her friend with the truck showed up at my door. Dolly's friend, Melvin, was a very nice guy as well. The assistant manager of the apartment, Mr. B., had allowed me to keep the apartment one more day so I would be able to get my furniture out. Dolly's friend, Melvin, and another one of his friends, Joshua, took control of moving my furniture out of the apartment.

That was a very sad time for me, but I must remember I brought all of that on myself; there was no one to blame but me. After they moved all of the big, heavy furniture out of the place, I still had many valuable items left, my personal things—ten years' worth. There were a lot of things that I could not replace, pictures and gifts that I had received from dear friends before my addiction had started. There were people, for example, coworkers, church people, and folks that I could have considered friends, but I did not want them to see me in the condition I was in, being a very serious drug addict. I went through a very rough time, not knowing that the worst was yet to come.

There was a laundry room that was not in use right off to the left of my three-bedroom apartment. That was the place where Mr. B stored all my valuable things, all the things that I could not get into my car. That's where they were stored, in the broken-down laundry room where the only lock was a rusted chain, and God knows who had a key to that old rusted chain. And again, that was no one's fault but mine. There is an old saying that goes like this: "When you smile, the whole world smiles with you. But when you cry, you will cry alone." That is true in my findings. It is true.

Let me tell you something, if you got everything in your life going pretty smooth, let well enough alone. You can live well without ever starting to use drugs or alcohol. If you just have so much money that you need to find something to spend it on, use it wisely. If you have a family, spend it on something that you and your family can enjoy. If you are single, spend your money wisely. Spend it on something that you can fall back on. Because, believe it or not, there will be a rainy day that happens in all of our lives at one time or another. Don't be caught out in the rain with nothing. People, please wake up and stop being stupid! After Mr. B. moved all my personal things out into the old broken-down laundry room outside to the left of my apartment, it had begun to get dark, and all of those old so-called friends had gone inside their warm apartments and left me and my two children outside in the cold. Mr. B. had locked up my apartment with some of my remaining personal property still inside. These were things that I said that I would be back the next day to get, knowing all the time that I had no place to take them.

I was very blessed that Dolly Dimple and Angie were kind enough to take my big furniture in. Getting a storage place was out of the question. There was no money for that. Period. So here is the killer. After Mr. B. locked us out, we were just standing in the hallway hugging each other and just crying together, lost with no place to go. Like I said, it was nobody's fault but mine. Gwendolyn did not live too far from us. So I decided to go down by Gwendolyn's house to sit for a moment until I figured out where we were going after becoming homeless. We walked over to Gwendolyn's apartment and knocked on the door. It took a long time for them to come to the door. Gwendolyn and Ben were the couple that could not wait until I got home every evening so they could come over and eat, drink, get high, and listen to music all night long, free of charge. I kept knocking for about five more minutes. After they realized that we were not going to leave, Gwendolyn finally came to the door.

I said, "Hi, Gwen, we just decided we would come and sit by you and Ben until we decide what our next move will be."

Gwendolyn plainly said, "Geraldine, I am sorry for what just happened to you and your family, but Ben told me to tell you that we are not having any company tonight or tomorrow. But I will see you around."

My knees buckled. I was so overwhelmed that I felt as though I was about to pass out. But I just stood there like a silly little fool, practically penniless with no place to go. That was one of the biggest blows that I had felt all through my addiction, not realizing that the worst was still to come. So we went out and got into my car. I took my younger child down to Sweet Sadie's house, and my older child got back into my car, and we hit the freeway and drove until we could not drive any farther. We stopped at a convenience store and purchased all kinds of food, snacks, and drinks. We ended up at a drive-in theater in the Valley. We paid our way in and watched a movie that we really did not care about because it didn't matter. All we wanted was some place safe to get some rest. We started to watch the movie, and we ate until we got so full that we could not move. It was a blessing that we were in the car sitting down; otherwise, we would have been in trouble. We watched the movie and fell asleep. When I woke up the next morning, approximately six in the morning, my child was on the backseat of my car, and I was on the front seat of my car, and there was no one in that drive-in theater lot but us.

I thought to myself, *How were we able to sleep through the night like this?* Then I thought, *It had to be God.* So we got ourselves together as much as we could in the car, and we drove around the neighborhood in the Valley. There we found it to be very pleasing to us. We checked out a few apartment buildings that had "For Rent" signs on them, and we put in a few applications to see if we qualified to get one of the apartments. I had a little over one thousand dollars in my possession that I had saved from that lump sum of money that I had received approximately two months earlier. I should have had more, but I had been so stupid spending the rest on the guttersnippers who did not mean us any good, none whatsoever.

So we rode around for approximately two days, stopping in and asking the managers of the apartments where we had applied if we were approved for the apartment due to the fact that we did not have a telephone number where we could receive a call concerning the application. After two days had gone by, we stopped at one of the apartments we had applied for, and the manager told us, "Yes, you can have the apartment."

We shouted for joy! The manager wanted eight hundred dollars total to move in. The security deposit was included. How happy were we!

We had all our necessities in our car. For example, blankets, TV, pots and pans, toiletries, everything that we really needed. The apartment came with central heating, central air, a stove, and a refrigerator. We were set up. We had a little over two hundred dollars left after paying all our expenses; we were some happy campers. After we got settled into the one-bedroom apartment, we went to the grocery market and just filled the cabinets and refrigerator up.

We got inside that apartment and turned the heater and the little black-and-white TV on. We were so happy we felt as if we were in heaven. The only thing that was missing was my other child. So we soon drove back to Los Angeles and got him. We had our own home one more time.

So we lived comfortably in our new place without a problem. One day, I decided to drive to Los Angeles to see who had moved into my old apartment. I went up to the door and knocked. Guess who came to the door? It was Samantha.

I said, "Hi, Samantha. What are you doing here?"

Samantha said, "What in the hell do you think? I live here, b———. When you had this nice place, you did not know what in the hell to do with it. Now, b———, I am going to show you how a real b——— lives in a nice place like this. Oh yes, by the way, get the f——— away from my door!"

I almost passed out. You could have bought me for a plug nickel. I was outdone—overwhelmed. I was beside myself. I felt like a stupid little fool. But again, it was no one's fault but mine. Totally stupidity on my part; I had no one to blame but myself. I was so upset to the point that I wanted some answers. So I went down to the manager's office and asked for Mr. B., the assistant manager. Mr. B. walked up to the counter and said, "Yes, Ms. Thomas, how can I help you?"

I said, "Mr. B., why did you rent my old apartment to Samantha?"

He said, "Ms. Thomas, she earned it." "Earned it how?" I asked.

He replied, "You know how every day she was sitting down in your apartment talking with you? Well, Ms. Thomas, everything that went on in your life during that time, Samantha reported it back to this office. That was one of our main tools that we used for evicting you. The last report we got from Samantha on you was a seven-page letter, and that is what tied the knot, Ms. Thomas. I am sorry for you and your family, but I hope you have learned a lesson from this."

I dropped my head and walked out of the manager's office. There was nothing more for me to say.

People, people, please wake up and stop being stupid! When you have someone on your heels, asking you a bunch of questions, wanting to know what makes you tick, how you are making it, who you are involved with, who you communicate with, when you leave home, where do you go, who do you go with, how much you paid for everything you have, who is most important to you as a spouse, who you trust the most, well, some people would call these stupid questions, but you need to stop and think that this person is after what you have; and if you keep slipping, they will have it. Wake up and smell the coffee before it turns into tea. This is why I have a problem with people saying they took what you had; that's a lie. *You* gave it away. Stop blaming people for your stupid mistakes. Stand up and take responsibility for your own stupidity because that is the only way you can solve the problem. Keep your damn mouth shut about your business because the less people know about you, the better off you are. Now go figure.

After I found out how I had been crossed by one of my best friends, my whole demeanor changed. However, it did not change enough because I did not get completely sober. I went back to my apartment in the Valley and began to drink like a fish. It was out-of- control drinking. I was thinking about how big of a fool I had been and how long I had been a big fool on a continued basis. I would drink daily. The reason I was able to drink so much and so regularly was because the new apartment complex that I moved into had a lot of people who would drink all day long, from early in the morning until late at night. All they did was drink and invite me over to join them, which I was happy to do without a problem because I was still a serious alcoholic and drug addict.

Chapter 6

Using Drugs and Alcohol
Is a Road to Hell

I was doing okay for months, just drinking like a fish, until my cousin came to California from Tennessee to visit me. I had been living drug-free in our new apartment in the Valley for approximately one year and had not thought about buying any drugs.

I will call my cousin Felton. On the day Felton arrived at my apartment, the first thing he said was, "Cousin, where is the glass pipes? I got the crack."

Felton had approximately five hundred dollars' worth of crack cocaine in a plastic sandwich bag. When I looked down and saw that crack in that sandwich bag, I forgot about my sobriety. All I could think about was *Where in the hell can I find a brand-new glass pipe?* That was the only thing on my mind. I had totally relapsed the moment I saw that plastic bag. It was over for me. I could kiss good-bye to everything I had worked so hard for because it was on and crackin'.

Not only did Felton bring approximately five hundred dollars' worth of crack with him, but he also had about two thousand dollars in his wallet. Do I have to tell you what happened to that two grand? Well, yes, you are right! Felton spent the majority of the remaining money on crack as well. We found a little dope spot about one block and a half from where I lived, and we wore it out. How stupid could I be? This is what you call insanity. People, people, wake up and stop being stupid. If you are a drug user, and if you have made up your mind to stop using it, I don't care if it is your mother who knocks on your door. If she has drugs in her possession, turn her away. This is how you will know that you are finished with drugs and anyone who uses them. If you open your door for someone with drugs, and you know they have drugs, and you welcome them into your home, this could only mean one thing—and that is, you had relapsed before the knock ever came upon the door. This is one reason I don't blame Felton for my starting to use drugs again. I got that smoke party started quickly. That is how I know I had relapsed before Felton ever knocked on my door. People, people, wake up and stop being stupid. Life is too short to live like a sucker. Don't do this to yourself and your family. You have as much right as anyone else to live a clean and sober life. That is your right, just as many other things are. Don't be cheated out of it. Don't allow this to happen to you. Put God first and allow Him to win this battle for you.

Long before Felton got to my home, I had got my furniture from Dolly. And Dolly and Angie had got themselves some new furniture as well. When I got my furniture back, it was in very good condition. They took very good care of it; I was very pleased and thankful about how well they kept my furniture. When Felton arrived at my door, my apartment was looking very nice. You could not tell that it had been less than a year since I had been evicted from my last apartment. So when Felton got there, my apartment was already fixed up. I thought I was ready and could handle a big crack cocaine party. How mistaken I was. Everything went well for a few months. But once I started getting loaded off crack cocaine, and I had never quit drinking alcohol, all hell broke loose. I went stone crazy.

People, people, please wake up and stop being stupid! Wakeup and smell the coffee before it turns into tea. People, please, please listen to me, and let me tell you something: When you are trying to get off drugs, you cannot drink alcohol. If you are trying to recover from drugs, the success rate of staying off drugs is very low if you are drinking. All alcohol does is carry you right back into your drug addiction.

Now let me be clear. When you stop using drugs, you will say, "I am so happy that I am not using drugs anymore. I have finally got that monkey off my back." But listen, please listen to me; when you pick that paraphernalia up again, whatever kind you may use, your drug addiction will be a million times worse than it was when you put it down. When you first put your addiction down, you called it a monkey; but I guarantee you that when you pick it back up again, if you dare, it will be a big-ass gorilla, and don't let anyone tell you any differently. And let me tell you another thing: When you have been clean and off drugs for about a year—or however long you have been off drugs, you know how long it took you to get to where you were when you stopped, as they say, "Tore down from the floor down and had hit rock bottom." Well, let me be clear again, you will get all of the back and more in a matter of days if you pick up again because the addiction is still there in your system waiting to be triggered. This is why they call it a recovering addict. Because all that drug needs is just a little spark, and that addiction will wake up so quickly that you will forget you were ever sober. And when it wakes up, it will kick your natural ass.

People, I cannot say this enough. If you have never tried drugs, please don't! Please save your life, dignity, and your good name. Because once you take your first hit or fix off a cocaine pipe or needle or whatever you may attempt to use, all of those things that I just named will be gone, and most of the time, you will not get them back. The number of addicts who die is much higher than the number of addicts who live. Now breathe into your nose and out through your mouth because this is some real shit to take in. If you want to be denied of your pride, dignity, morals, self-esteem, success in life, and a good future, hit that damn pipe, and I guarantee you that your dream will come to pass.

Life in the drug lane was good for me during the time Felton was there in my home because money kept coming in the house. Felton was a long-distance truck driver, and whenever money started to get low, Felton would sober up long enough to get a truck-driving job. After that, the party was on once again. I thought this was living. How mistaken I was! There is so much that happened to me and my family in between what I am telling you now, but I cannot tell it all in one book. So there will be more books to come, and the point is to help the suffering drug addicts to understand that they do not have to continue to live their lives like this. Recovery works, and God works even better. After about a year of continuing to get loaded with my cousin Felton and the other drug addicts that I met out in the Valley, I was right back where I cut off in Los Angeles, back at rock bottom one more time.

One evening, after hitting rock bottom, I went to the mailbox, and there was a letter in my mailbox from Louisiana addressed to me from my oldest sister. May God rest her soul. The letter was telling me where she was and what condition she was in. On the pages, you could see drops of blood that had dripped from her nose. She told me that it took her a few days to write that letter because every time she attempted to write me, her nose would start to bleed due to her very bad liver disease.

Samoan wrote in the letter, "Geraldine, I just wanted to write you and let you know how much I love you, and oh, how I miss you." She also wrote, "By the time you receive this letter, I might be gone, but before I go, I want you to know I love you."

I am crying right now as I write this section because I do believe today that if she had known that there was help out there for an alcoholic, she would have sought after it. But by this time, her liver was so badly damaged from drinking alcohol that it was beyond repair. Right after I read Samoan's letter, I rushed to the telephone and called the hospital in Louisiana where my oldest sister had written me from. When my call was answered, I asked the person on the other end for my sister, Samoan.

The person on the other end said, "Samoan who?" I said, "Samoan Thomas."

After the person on the other end of the telephone verified who I was and got a complete description of my sister, she said, "Miss, I am very sorry to have to tell you this, but Ms. Samoan Thomas passed away last night in her sleep."

When that lady told me that, I almost dropped the telephone. I became speechless. All I was thinking about was that I did not get a chance to tell my oldest sister that I loved her before she passed away. People, people, please wake up and stop being stupid, like waiting until it is too late to help your loved ones when you know they are suffering from an addiction that can and *will* kill them. Stop being too damn grand and great to tell a loved one that you love them whether they are addicted to a substance or not because just those three words can sometimes be a determining factor to whether they live or die. Breathe in through your nose and out through your mouth because this shit is real. Now go figure.

My children and I began to prepare to go to Mississippi to attend Samoan's funeral. We started by getting our apartment in great condition before leaving because we did not know how long we would be gone due to the fact that we were leaving with a very small amount of money. Our finances were nowhere intact. Therefore, we wanted our apartment to be in very good condition when we returned home, no matter how long that might be.

I finally got our bus fare together to leave for Mississippi to go to my sister's funeral. We were nowhere near airplane-fare ready. Very few poor cocaine addicts fly, you know, especially when they have no support in helping them to do so. I was the type of crack cocaine addict and alcoholic who had no good friends because I did not know how to pick them. I only knew how to pick guttersnippers.

If you don't know what I mean about *guttersnipper*, allow me to give you an example. I once had a male friend—I will call him Casper—that I thought was my real friend, to the point that he came to my home to visit me one evening. I had gotten my hands on a nice little piece of money, so this friend of mine came by; Caper was a guy that I used to get high with. When Casper came by my apartment, he brought a few cocaine rocks with him. My children were gone for the weekend. I had given them their spending money, and they were happy. They were in Los Angeles at the home of their godmother, Sweet Sadie. So Casper and I started talking, catching up on what had happened since we had last seen each other. A lot can happen in an addict's life in no time, especially when they travel in the same circle. It was a lot to talk about. So after we finished talking and catching up on things, Casper pulled out his plastic bag and said, "I have a few crack rocks. If you like, we can smoke them. I did not have any money to get the drinks, so I just brought the crack to see what you were doing."

I said, "Cool, I have a few dollars to get the drinks." Casper said, "Cool."

I then said, "Well, if you don't mind, will you go to the store and pick up some drinks before we get started? I have some drinks here, but not that much."

Casper said, "Yes, I will go because once we get started on getting high, we are not going to want to stop and go to the store for drinks."

I said, "Cool."

I gave him a twenty-dollar bill. Casper laid the dope sack on the table, and he went on to the store that was right on the corner from the house, not far at all. I could hardly wait for Casper to get back because I wanted to get started, especially with the dope sack lying right on my table. I was pacing the floor as though I had already hit the pipe. I hadn't had anything that day. Just the thought of it kept me going.

Casper finally made it back from the store with the drinks, and the party was on. We stayed at that table for two days, using my money, going in and out to buy drugs and alcohol. Casper would be the one I trusted to go score everything, drugs and alcohol. We did not need any food because I had plenty of food in my refrigerator. I fed him anything he wanted to eat, which wasn't that much. When you are smoking crack, the appetite is very limited. So finally, around the end of the smoke party, I had laid some money down on the table, not thinking anything because everything had been going smoothly. So I got up and went to the restroom. After I returned, the money was not there. It was gone.

So I said, "Casper, I laid some money down on the table before going to the restroom. Now it is not there. Do you know what happened to it?"

Casper said, "No, I have not seen it."

I said, "That's strange. I know I am loaded and tired, but I am not crazy."

Casper said, "Well, let's look for it."

I was being stupid, so I said, "Okay." We were down, crawling around on the floor looking for the money. I looked over to ask Casper a question, and in Casper's pants pocket, there was some money hanging out. He did not push the money all the way in his pocket. So I asked Casper, "Casper, how much money do you have? Maybe you can buy the next rock."

Casper said, "You know, I told you when I first got here. I do not have any money."

I said, "That is what I know." I snatched my money from his pockets and said, "Now give me the rest of my money out of your pocket! You have been in my home for the last two days. I have treated you like a brother. I have trusted you with my home, my money, and my life, and you turn around and steal from me? I was down on my knees looking for my money, sweating, and you were down on your knees looking and sweating harder than I was when you knew all the time you had stolen my money, and it was in your pocket. Man, you get up and leave my home right now, and don't you ever come back again with your guttersnipping ass."

This is what I mean when you hear me say *guttersnipper*. There is a lot of this going on in the drug-using world. There is no such thing as fair play. It does not exist, especially when you are dealing with some broke, poor drug addicts and alcoholics. People, people, please wake up and stop being stupid. You will not be successful using drugs and alcohol. You will not win. Addiction is a osing game no matter how you look at it. The drug game is for losers. It may seem as though you are winning for a minute, but before the game is over, you will find out that you are just another loser.

Now back to our bus trip to Mississippi.

My friend Jordan had moved to the Valley also. As a matter of fact, he moved out there before I did. So after we got packed up and ready to go, I called Jordan and told him that we were ready to leave for Mississippi and would he come over and take us to the bus station. Jordan, being the faithful friend he was, said he would be right over. Now, people, don't get it twisted or misunderstand what I am saying. There are some real, true friends in this world. But as I said earlier in this book, a friend is like a diamond; they are very precious and very rare. So when you find one, you better hold on to them because they very seldom come along.

Jordan came over to my apartment, picked us up, and took us to the bus station. He waited until we got on the bus before he left. When our bus pulled off, Jordan was waving good-bye to us. We were off on our long journey to Mississippi, a place I hadn't been in years, mostly due to my addiction. I was ashamed to be seen in my own hometown because I had fallen from sugar to shit in a matter of five years.

A family member picked us up from the bus station. When he looked and saw the way I looked, he did not say anything, but I saw the expression on his face change; I knew I looked like hell. But he was still nice to us, so we went on to get unpacked. My sister's funeral was going to be the following day. It took us about a week to get there after we heard the news. The following day, we went to the funeral. We walked up to view my sister's body, and when I got to her casket and looked down at her, she looked like someone that I had never seen before in my life. Alcohol had eaten her poor little body up. May God rest her soul. I was one out-of-control drug addict looking down at a deceased alcoholic; we were two sisters who loved each other dearly. My heart was just torn apart. As

I looked down at my sister, I thought about how I could have helped her. And at the same time, I was wondering, *How can I help myself?*

People, that was painful. My hands were tied. I also was thinking that the way my life was going, I just might be next.

People, people, please wake up and stop being stupid because when you become an out-of-control alcoholic and addict, there are only a few places you will end up, and that is in jail, in a mental intuition, or in the morgue. Like I said, being an addict is a losing game—no win, no way. Breathe in through your nose and out through your mouth because this shit is real. I will not go into everything that went on in Mississippi while we were there because that is a book by itself.

So we stayed in Mississippi for a while. Finally, we returned back home to California. We were very happy to be home again. I called Jordan up and told him we were back in Los Angeles at the bus station, and I asked him if he would please come and give us a ride home. He asked where we were. I told him where, and Jordan said he would be right there. I said, "Okay."

We waited for a little while, then Jordan arrived. We were very happy to finally be on our way home. I know you have heard this quote before, "There is no place like home." We were riding the freeway, laughing and talking, just happy to be home again.

We finally arrived at our home. When we got there, we found all our furniture chopped up and in the big green Dumpster. I almost passed out. My children just broke down and started crying like newborn babies. I had to fish through the Dumpster to get my family pictures out. Some of them were ripped in half. There were sliding glass doors on my apartment that had been taken completely off and broken. All you had to do was just step inside my apartment. I went from neighbor to neighbor and asked them, "Do you know what happened to our home?" Each and every one of them said no, they did not hear or see anything. The last place I went to that night was the manager's apartment to ask if she knew what happened to my apartment.

She said no as well. My rent was paid up, so I know it was not an eviction. I would not have taken that chance. But one strange thing happened that night in the manager's apartment. I looked in the manager's bedroom, and there was one of my children's baby pictures standing on their end table.

I walked over, picked the picture up, and asked the manager, "How did this picture get in here?"

She said, "I saw this picture out by the Dumpster, and I thought this would be something you would want."

Again, I was blown away. Up to this day, I never did find out who vandalized my apartment. Jordan was still there with us during the time we were looking at our vandalized home, and he said, "I don't have a very large place, but if you don't mind that, you can come and go home with me. You are welcome to stay with me until you can find another place, and I will help you to do just that."

Jordon stood by us until we found another place to live, and we moved on from that segment in our lives to the next one.

Chapter 7

Drugs and Alcohol Do
Not Discriminate

After we moved out of Jordan's home into our own home, we were living independently once again. While we were staying with Jordan, I remained sober because he did not use any drugs. He was a clean- cut guy, very respectable, and a very good friend.

Jordan always told me, "Geraldine, I wish you would not use drugs. You and your little children deserve better than that. Your capabilities are much greater than what you give yourself credit for."

Every time Jordan said those words to me, I gave him a big hug and said, "You are my big brother that my mother never had, and I love you just that way. Thank you, Jordan, for being the person that you are." I lived in the Valley for two years after my home was vandalized.

During that time, I was blessed with another child. Right after the birth of my new child, I moved back to Los Angeles, which was another one of the biggest mistakes I ever made in my entire life—again.

When I moved back to Los Angeles, I was blessed to be reinstated on my job—again. That's where I met this young man. I will call him Diaz. Diaz was from Texas. He was a smooth-talking country boy. He thought I was a needy recovering drug addict, and I thought he was too. Diaz and I started dating. I knew Diaz was an alcoholic, but I did not know he was an active cocaine addict, which in many ways proved to be very bad for me.

In the beginning of our relationship, Diaz treated me very well, like a little princess. Since we worked together, every evening we made a stop at the liquor store to buy a case of beer. We started off buying six packs and eventually graduating to buying cases. I had a nice car. We sat out in front of my home drinking beer and talking about sex for hours.

It seemed as if I got stuck on being stupid when it came to Diaz. I could not get my head straight for nothing. I was always thinking about that man to the point that it seemed as if I put Diaz before my family. I started to do stupid things, things that were out of the ordinary like letting him spend some nights in my home where my family lived. That wasn't cool at all, but I let my weakness take over what I knew was wrong. That's when I knew I had started slipping again.

A little while after that first night he spent at my home, I found out he was a crack addict. I had been using off and on after I moved out of Jordan's home, but it wasn't regularly—as if that makes it okay. It doesn't! Either you are a crackhead or you are not. There is nothing in between. Now go figure. People, wake up and stop being stupid. Let me tell you something: two crackheads together cannot do anything but smoke crack and take each other down in the gutter. I don't care how many assets you two start out with, if you keep playing the crack game, you will sink like a ship with a hole in it. If you think I am lying, just try it. Wait! I don't like telling you to try it because I know what it will do. Please, take my word for it. I am not telling you what I think. I am telling you what *I know*. You better wake up and smell the coffee before it turns into tea because this shit is real. Drugs will kick your natural ass and ask you how many more times you want to be kicked. Not only will it kick your ass, it will kill you. This is the whole idea. Please don't allow this to happen to you. I have seen it happen too many times.

After I let Diaz spend the first few nights at my home and allowed him to sleep in my bed with me, the man began to lose respect for me. He did not seem as interested as he did before. I let my little needy feelings take over and allowed him to sleep in my home. Don't misunderstand me. Every man is not like Diaz. There are some men who can be given that privilege and will rise to the occasion. However, you must listen to what I said. I said, "Man, not a crackhead!" They don't give a damn about anybody but themselves. Diaz had gotten to where he stopped riding with me and started to ride with a coworker who was from Texas as well. The reason he allowed me to give him a ride sometimes was because he needed to go by and see his sick father. That worked until one evening when I decided to take something to his daddy's house that he had left in my car. I thought he might have needed it. Do you know what his sick daddy told me?

He said, "Geraldine, I haven't seen Diaz in two months. If you see him before I do, will you please tell him I would like to see him?"

I said, "Mr. Diaz, I will do that for you. Before I leave, is there anything I can do for you?"

Mr. Diaz said, "No, baby, thank you. I just want to see my son.

If you can help me with that, I sure would appreciate it."

I said, "I promise you, I will do everything I can to make that possible."

As I walked away, I was feeling like a natural-born fool because I had put myself in that position, not Diaz. You should never go looking for a person unannounced. I got exactly what I deserved, nothing more, and nothing less.

Diaz would talk about Texas, saying he wanted to go back home, but I never thought too much about it. I thought he was just talking. One Friday, we got paid, and Diaz said he was going by his daddy's house. He asked me to come by later and pick up some money he had for me. I said "Okay." That evening, I went by Diaz's house, and you know what happened? Diaz's dad said, "Geraldine, he didn't tell you?"

I said, "No, Mr. Diaz, tell me what?"

"Baby, Diaz left here about three hours ago headed to Texas. He and one of his coworkers are driving there. They are way up the road by now. I am so sorry he didn't tell you, but Diaz does things like this quite often. I am very sorry that you had to find out this way."

I felt as though I could have fallen through that floor. That's how hurt, shocked, and ashamed I was at that news. I felt like a fool once again.

I left Mr. Diaz's home, and instead of going to my home, I went straight to the dope house and bought myself a big crack rock, sat down, and smoked it. Then I was off and running one more time, and I had no place to go. I spent my paycheck that night.

The following Saturday morning, I was still sitting in the dope house, dead broke, and a few minutes from being kicked out of the dope house, where I had just spent my last dime. When your money is gone, baby, you got to go, no doubt about it. You have to shake the spot. You may not have to go home, but you have to leave there. Please believe me. It is no lie. Please wake up and stop being stupid. Wake up and smell the coffee before it turns into tea because this shit is real. Now go figure.

I finally got myself together enough to get up and leave the dope house. I was penniless. I did not have a dime to my name. I was overwhelmed with shame and sadness. I made it home. When I walked into the house, I did not have too much to say. I was very quiet due to the guilt I was carrying in my soul. I stayed inside the rest of the weekend and returned to work Monday morning with a lot of grief I had brought on myself. How stupid could I have been? I went on with that routine for about six months, and I fell off the wagon one more time.

After I fell off the wagon, and right before I lost my home, Diaz sent me and my baby a ticket to come to Texas. After a few more runs, I decided to take the bus and head out to Texas. It was, again, one of the biggest mistakes I ever made in my life. As you continue to read this book, you will discover that I made quite afew mistakes—big mistakes—in my lifetime, mistakes I truly regret. If I could change and rethink some of the decisions that I made during my lifetime, I would do it in a heartbeat. I am so very sorry that I allowed my life to take such horrible turns because it happened just like I said. I allowed these things to happen to me. No one did this to me. I did it to myself. I had some people who encouraged me to do the wrong things, but at the end of the day, I made the decisions that affected my life.

Life is about choices, and the choice is yours to make. Therefore, this is where these quotes come into play: "Life is what you make it" and "It is what it is." It is about taking responsibility today. Take responsibility for your own actions and move on. That is what I had to do in order to get any type of healing. I had to stop placing blame on everybody but myself. When I did that, that's when I began to heal. You have to face the music. You may not like what you hear, but you must play the tape all the way through before you can begin to be healed. People, people, please stop being stupid. Wake up and smell the coffee.

So I eventually arrived in Texas at Diaz's home where we settled into what was going to be our new home for a long time. At that time, I will go as far as to say we planned that Diaz's home was going to be our home forever. When we arrived at the bus station, Diaz had one of his family members to pick us up—a super-nice person whom I hold dear to my heart even up until this day. His family member picked us up from the bus station because Diaz had to work that day. Diaz did not own a car; therefore, he had to have someone to pick us up. That should have been a sign right there that we were in the wrong place. So we arrived at Diaz's home. I went right to work, trying to make that house a home. The family member that picked us up at the bus station, I will call her Cynthia. Cynthia had a great way about her that was truly, truly awesome, one that I will never forget. What a beautiful person she was to us. Cynthia stayed with us at Diaz's house until he got home from work, which was very much appreciated.

Upon our arrival in Diaz's home, he treated us nicely, as though he was very happy that we were there. That went on for approximately three months.

Before I left for Texas, I mentioned to Sweet Sadie that I was thinking about going to Texas, and the circumstances that I was going under.

She said, "Baby, please don't do that! That is one thing that a woman should never do. And that is to leave the state where she lives to follow a man to another state, which is his hometown. That would be one of the biggest mistakes you could ever make in your life."

Well, I didn't listen to Sweet Sadie, as you know. I followed my own bad decision-making as usual and went on to Texas. After being in Texas for about three months, Diaz's attitude started to change toward us, slowly but surely. Diaz's patterns began to change. He started to hang out with his friends up until two or three o'clock in the morning every chance he got, at least that is what he told me. After we were there for approximately six months, I received some money. It was a nice amount, enough to purchase a nice car. Because I did not have any Texas identification, I decided it would be okay to register the car in Diaz's name. That was another big mistake. So on the same evening that I purchased the car, it seemed as though Diaz got very angry after we left the car lot. I could not do anything to please him. Everything I said or did made him frown. I had two hundred dollars left after I bought the car, and that money was for my baby. So I had Diaz take us by the mall so I could do some shopping for my baby. Diaz pulled up to the mall, and the first thing he said was "I will wait for you in the car."

We went into the mall, and I spent the last two hundred dollars on my baby. We had quite a few bags when we came out of the store. We walked over to where the car was parked, but neither the car nor Diaz was there. So we waited around for thirty to forty-five minutes, and finally, Diaz pulled up.

I said, "Diaz, where did you go? We have been standing out here a long time waiting for you."

Diaz said, "Oh, I just drove around to my cousin's house so I could show him our car."

It was raining and cold, so we were pretty wet when we got into the car. Diaz started to act very peculiar. He got very angry, and suddenly, he said, "Why in the hell you ask me where I been? I am grown. I can go anywhere I want to go. Don't you start that shit because I will show you something."

I said, "Show me what? What is wrong with you? I only asked you where you were when we came out of the store because we were standing out here in the rain."

Diaz said, "You should have took your ass back in the store and waited until I got back."

I said, "Why are you carrying on like this? I just asked you one question."

Diaz was driving while we were talking. Then he pulled over to the side of the road, jumped out of the car, came around to the passenger's side of the car, snatched open the car door, and said, "Bitch, I am going to show you right now who's in charge of this family."

My baby was still in the backseat of the car screaming, "Leave my mommy alone! Stop hitting my mommy!"

All I could concentrate on was my baby. The car was still running, and I was afraid she would try to get out of the car and come to me. I was screaming, "Stay in the car, baby, don't get out! Please, stay in the car!"

We were downtown in front of a very tall building. I could hear people driving by yelling, "Leave that lady alone!" Someone said, "Stop beating that lady like that. I am calling the police right now!" Diaz beat me a while longer, and when he was about through using his fists, he stood up and raised his foot right over my head. By that time, a man was standing beside him, and that man said, "If you do, I will kill you right here."

To show you that Diaz was a coward, he looked at that man and walked back to the car that I had just bought, got in it, and drove off with my baby.

The man said, "Don't worry! The police got the license plate number. They will catch him."

The man helped me to stand and asked if I was all right. I said, "Yes, I just want my baby."

By that time, two police cars pulled up. One car went after Diaz, and the other stayed with me. The man who helped me, his car was parked in the street. After the police arrived, he got back in his car and left. I told the police that the man was not a witness; that he stopped to help me.

Within a couple of minutes, and while the police was taking my statement, the other police car returned to the scene with Diaz and my baby. I ran to my child to see if she was okay. I told the police that I had just purchased that car today. However, Diaz said, "This is my car! This car is in my name."

I told the police that Diaz was telling a lie, that I had just received some money that very same day in the mail, and I had my receipt to prove where I had cashed my check. Plus, I had the bill of sale to the car in my purse. I told the officers that I had just recently moved to Texas about six months ago, and I hadn't had a chance to get my driver's license yet, and that's the reason the car was in Diaz's name.

I said, "Officer, the plan was that as soon as I got my driver's license, we would change the title and put the car in my name. And this man has the nerve to stand here and say to my face, and in front of you officers, that my car is his. The reason why I bought the car is for family purposes. Diaz had someone to pick him up every morning at four o'clock to give him a ride to work. I thought it would be a nice idea if Diaz could drive himself to work. Maybe he would not have to get up so early. But this is the thanks I get— again."

So the policeman said to Diaz, "Man, why don't you stop lying? You know as well as I do that this car was bought with this lady's money, wasn't it?"

That's when Diaz said, "Yes, sir, officer. She paid for the car. It's hers."

The officer said, "Diaz, you know you left with Ms. Thomas's child in the car. Therefore, we can book you on two charges. And they are battery and kidnap. What you think about that?"

Diaz said, "That won't look too good for me."

The officer responded by saying, "Earlier, it did not look too good for Ms. Thomas, did it?" Diaz said, "No, it didn't."

The policeman went on to say, "Now turn around and put your hands behind your back because I am going to take you to jail."

The policeman went on to say, "Geraldine, I want you to show up in court Monday morning to press charges on Diaz. If you don't show up, I will personally come out to your house and arrest you myself."

Then the officer went on to say, "Can you drive? Can you find your way back to the house where you live?"

I said, "Yes, sir, I know how to get home."

The officer directed me to drive straight down the street until I got to Seventeenth Street and turn left. Then continue to drive until I passed Broadway and continue on. Then I would arrive at my address. I thanked the officer and told him I would be in court on Monday morning.

First of all, I had no business following that man to his hometown. As a matter of fact, I had no business following that man no place after the way he treated me here in Los Angeles. Let me tell you something, folks. A leopard doesn't change its spots, only rearranges them. If it looks like a guttersnipper, walks like a guttersnipper, acts like a guttersnipper, and smells like a guttersnipper, nine times out of ten, it is a damn guttersnipper. I got into the car and drove off, supposedly going to my home, but instead, I passed the street that I live on, and at that time, I decided to turn left and go to Cynthia's home.

When I arrived at Cynthia's home, I became very sad and started to cry hysterically. That's when I remembered that I had intentionally put away some money in the house. That's when I asked Cynthia to babysit my child while I went over to Diaz's to pick up something. She immediately said, "Yes."

As I prepared to leave Cynthia's home, my thoughts weren't clear. I had some nasty thinking going on. All I had in my mind was that I wanted to smoke some crack cocaine at any cost; no matter what it would take, I was willing to go to any length. As I walked out of Cynthia's door, it was raining very hard, and it was cold. Cynthia lived far out in the country where there were few streetlights, and therefore, it was very dark. I could barely see my hand before my face. My knees and elbows were still bleeding from Diaz dragging me from the car I had purchased that day, and so stupidly put the title of the car in someone else's name. How stupid could I be?

As I sit here today, I think of how immature I was, thinking of buying transportation that I was unable to put in my name, before I went shopping for my child and myself. I really had my priorities twisted.

As I was saying, all I could think about was getting high on some crack. The beating that Diaz had given me was an excuse to activate my addiction that I had so obviously subdued. All I needed was an excuse, and Diaz gave me one. So again, I was off and running, chasing that mirage one more time, one that I was all too familiar with, one that I knew would never have any satisfaction that would come out of it. So I drove back to the house where I was staying with Diaz and got the money that I had put away for a rainy day, not knowing that I really was going to need it on a rainy day, literally. People, people, please listen to me, and let me tell you something: One thing for sure will happen. If you are a hope-to-die, cold-blooded, out-of-control drug addict, geography does not work when you are trying to get away from a drug addiction because if you are a real or true drug addict—it doesn't matter what state you travel to—you will find that dope spot. It's a given; it just stands out like a sore thumb. You don't even have to go looking for it. It will find you. This is just how demonized drugs are.

Crack cocaine was one of the worst drugs that I had ever tried in my life. If you have never tried it, don't! Crack will make a ho out of a schoolteacher. Crack cocaine doesn't give a damn about who you are or how much money you have. It will take all of your dignity and destroy you, all in one hit. This is one thing about crack: it does not discriminate.

Near the home where I lived with Diaz, I had spotted the dope house early on just by going back and forth to the grocery store. Every other day as I traveled on foot going to the store, I passed a set of apartments where a group of people always stood. I don't care what time of day or night I passed that building, I always saw some of the same people hanging out and looking lost. As soon as a car drove up, about twenty people would jump all over it. That is a sure sign right there. Take it from me; been there, done that. That was when I said to myself, "I have just located the dope spot."

People, people, please wake up and stop being stupid. Wakeup and smell the coffee before it turns into tea. Whenever you come to a scene that looks like what I just described, one should tuck their tail and run like hell because if you stop and check it out, that could be one of the biggest mistakes you could ever make in your life. That one stop could send you on a run that could take you the rest of your life to get out of. Some never get out of it until death takes them out.

Well, after getting the money I had put away in Diaz's home, I was off and running straight down to the dope house that was located right up the street from my home. The dope spot was so close to where I lived that I left the car at home and walked down the street to the spot. It was only about two blocks away at the most. As I walked down the street to my destination, it began to get really scary. It was one o'clock on a Saturday morning, and every now and then, a car would drive by. Being from Los Angeles, at that time of the morning, people were just getting ready to party, so that part was creepy with the streets being almost bone dry. When I arrived at my destination, there were these same people standing out in front of the dope house as I expected.

People, people, please listen to me: Now that I think about it, the only reason I went by that place every other day to buy groceries was because I had already relapsed in my head. I just hadn't taken the first hit in Texas. All that was missing was the reason. That's all I needed. And Diaz gave me that reason when he beat me that rainy night in Texas.

I asked some of the regulars in front of the dope house whom I could score some crack from. I got help and advice from many drug users that was out there. By my being experienced in how it worked at the drug spot, I knew not to put my money in anyone's hands. So what I said was "I have a hundred dollars to spend, but I need to get inside and see who I am spending my money with."

A young man asked me, "You are not the cops, are you?" I said, "No."

By this time, one of Diaz's neighbors stepped up and said, "I know her. She is cool. She is my neighbor." That was my ticket to get inside.

Once inside, I discovered that there was no working electricity, only candles burning. I was ready to get my smoke on; I did not have any time to waste. After I bought the crack cocaine, it seemed as if everyone who was in their own little corner smoking, was starting to migrate to my corner—since

I was alone, I guess. I seemed like a pushover, but that was one thing I wasn't because I had just gotten the beating of a lifetime, so I felt one more would not hurt. I was ready for anything they were going to come with. The man of the house was a tall, light-skinned young man who wore his hair in dreadlocks. He had a thin build and wore a nice silk smoking jacket with matching slippers. He had light-brown eyes, and his fingernails were freshly manicured. Overall, the man was very well put together. So after he recognized that I seemed to be taken advantage of by the crew, he said, "Welcome to my home. May I ask you your name?"

I said, "Yes, my name is Jerri."

He said, "You are welcome to my home. If there is anything you need, please feel free to let me know."

I said, "Sure, thank you."

So I smoked until five o'clock that following morning until I got down to my last twenty dollars. That's when I decided to leave, go home, and smoke that last twenty at Diaz's house. I knew, deep down in my heart, I was on my way out. So I walked back down to the house, and that's when I realized that I did not have anything to smoke the crack with. So I went next door to this young man's apartment that I knew smoked crack just by looking at him. I asked him to come over to my house for a few minutes.

The young man said, "Yes, give me a few minutes, and I will be right over."

I returned home and waited for him to come over so I could ask him if I could use his pipe to smoke that twenty-dollar rock that I had just purchased.

Twenty minutes had passed, and a knock came upon the door. There stood a dark-skinned, short, stubby young man. His clothes were not too clean and were sort of hanging off him as if they were two sizes too big. Of course, Diaz was still in jail for the assault he had recently done on me. I asked the young man, Stephen, if he had any paraphernalia—a glass pipe that we could use to smoke with.

He said, "Sure, where is the dope?"

We sat there and smoked that last twenty-dollar rock of crack cocaine. After we finished, I said, "Well, Stephen, I guess that is all we have now. It is all gone. So I guess we will just call it a night."

Stephen said, "Okay, I guess I will see you around," and he left.

Now how stupid could I have been? That man knew Diaz was in jail and I was home alone. He had to be a decent man. As I sit back today and think about my actions back then, I could have lost my life to do some shit like that. Today, I would have gotten my throat cut or raped, and no one would have known who did it. I would have been another statistic. People, people, please wake up and stop being stupid. Wake up and smell the coffee before it turns into tea.

After I spent my money at the dope spot, I felt more stupid than I had felt in a long time. I had two things going that morning: a sore ass and empty pockets. How stupid could I have been? My head was hurting so bad because Diaz had pulled handfuls of hair out of my head. You could see bald spots where he had snatched my hair out without giving a damn. I lost my six months of sobriety that night. I relapsed to no end. It was ridiculous how I had allowed my life to be destroyed one more time.

When a person uses crack cocaine, they lose a lot. They lose their common sense and dignity. And please don't let me leave out one of the most important things we lose. More often than not, we lose our lives. Something that cannot be replaced!

People, please be mindful that if you never used crack cocaine and alcohol, please don't! It is not worth it. The price we have to pay is too great to even take that chance. And if you are a drug addict as we speak, please remember, it is not too late to change your lifestyle. You have just as much right as anyone else to live a sober and productive life. You must want your sobriety as bad or more than you wanted that high.

Warning and Healing

The way I found my healing was through my Higher Power whom I choose to call my Lord and Savior, Jesus Christ. He healed me! And I believe what he did for me, he will do for you if you just ask. But you must be real and consistent because this is not something you play with. Your life is on the line, something that is not replaceable. People, please think before you act because this shit is real. It is killing us every day.

Those who listen to the news and read newspapers know that drugs do not discriminate. It does not give a damn about who you are, how famous you are, how much money you have, or how poor you are. Drugs will take your ass out of here and never look back. People, we deserve better. Please listen, and stop being stupid. Prescription drugs are the number-1 killers today. If you think I am lying, check the records.

Another problem I had with myself concerning Diaz was that I always asked him, "Do you love me, baby?"

Stop that insane behavior, people. All that does is tear down your self-esteem. If a person loves you, the one thing you don't have to do is ask. If someone loves you, they will either tell you or show you. If they don't do either, then it is time for you to move on, kick rocks, because in a matter of minutes, the situation could get really ugly. There is no in between. They either do or they don't; that is the bottom line. Continuing to ask a person if they love you is very irritating. So, people, stop being dumb! I took a lot of hard hits before I got to where I am today. Most of it is very embarrassing and degrading stuff. I said I was never going to tell anyone about what I had gone through. I said it would be between me and my Higher Power. But then I thought about it. I thought about how God had saved my life, how His grace and mercy were so freely given to me, and how if it wasn't for the Lord, I would be dead today. I came too close to death too many times. So I decided to share my experience in hope that if it would just save one person from the hell I went through, it would be worth the shame and disgrace that I wear on my sleeve today.

After Stephen left my home early that Saturday morning, I was devastated one more time to the point that I just sat down and cried like a baby, uncontrollably, hopeless. After I finally got myself together as much as possible, I curled up in the bed and went to sleep. When I woke up again, it was that following Sunday morning, and I was totally destroyed. I had my mind fixed on what my next move would be, knowing that the following day was going to be Monday.

I was notified by the police on Friday night, after I was beaten so badly by Diaz, that if I did not show up in court to press charges against Diaz, they were going to come out to my house and arrest me. My mind was screwed up. *Where do I go from here?* I had given up everything I had in Los Angeles, which amounted to little or nothing. And I also knew that if I did not go to court, and Diaz was set free, I might as well be dead because I knew he was going to kill me. I also knew that if a man beat a woman like he did me, for nothing, I could only imagine what he would do to me for sending him to jail. So I sat there in that bed and racked my brain, which was all I could do. I had very little money left, and my baby was at Cynthia's house where I had left her on Friday night after the beating that Diaz gave me. I was running scared with no place to go. I would not wish that feeling on my worst enemy. That was a really bad feeling for anyone to have. I had gotten to this point by way of 1951 S. Drug Avenue, whether I wanted to face it or not. That was how my life had gotten to that point.

People, people, please listen! Stop being stupid! Wake up and smell the coffee before it turns into tea. If you never used drugs before in your life, please don't start. It will destroy you and everything you believe in. It will strip you butt-naked and leave you standing in the middle of the streets with no place to go. That's how cold that shit was.

I am trying to get your attention. I don't want you to have to go through all the torment that I went through. Take my word for it. Look around, listen to the news, read the newspapers, talk to your next-door neighbor. Please, talk to your children because if you forget to talk to your babies, someone else will remember to do so. And they might talk to them about something that you would have wished you discussed with them first. So don't wait too long to talk. So I began to collect my little items—some people call them belongings—around the house, and I started putting them in a box. Yes, that is what I said, a *box*. That is what I brought them to Texas in. The drugs had bitten me before I got to Texas, as you know. I went there to make a better life, a family for my child, Diaz, and me. However, my plan did not turn out like I had hoped. I began to pack. I had so many mixed emotions. I knew I was not going to court to press charges against Diaz because that was not what I went there for. The man had a place to live and had a job when we got there. It would not have given me any satisfaction for those things to be taken away from him along with his freedom. It was not his fault that he did not love me, and I made my move too soon.

People, listen to me; if someone loves you, they will not do anything intentionally to hurt you. There are no ifs, ands, or buts about it. They will not do it, male or female, bottom line. And if one day you find yourself in that situation, it is time to kick rocks. Meaning, get the hell out while the getting is available to you because some of us don't make it out alive. So I began little by little to put my belongings into that car that I had just purchased two days prior. I was like the boll weevil searching for a home. I was so exhausted that I would pack a little and lie down and rest a while, and then I would get up and start moving around again. That is a bad feeling, packing with no place to move. I finally called Cynthia and told her that I was okay, and if I did not make it there on Sunday, I would be there on Monday.

Cynthia said, "That's okay, Geraldine. Everything is okay here. Your baby is fine. She is happy and playing. I just want you to take care of yourself, and I want you to know that I will help you in every way I can."

I said, "Thank you, Cynthia. And I want to let you know that your kindness will never be forgotten."

Right now, as I sit here typing this, I cannot help but to cry because writing this brings back so many feelings I can never seem to escape. But today, I am still grateful inspite of everything that I have gone through. I am grateful for that man who got out of his car in the rain and walked over to my aid when Diaz stood over me to stomp me in my face, and said so softly to Diaz, "If you do, I will kill you right here."

Sir, wherever you are and whoever you are, I would like to say "Thank you! And first of all, I would like to thank God for sending you. There is no other way that could have happened

if it wasn't for the goodness of God, His grace, and mercy."
And to all those people who drove by and blew their car horns
and said, "Leave that lady alone!" I would like to say thanks to
you as well.

My baby was also screaming, "Leave my mommy alone!"
But I am so thankful that she did not get out of the car. For that
I am truly grateful.

First of all, young and old people, get educated because
self- preservation is the first law of the land. Learn how to
be independent, be able to take care of yourself and your
families legally. Learn how to do something that will benefit
you in life because, for the most part, if you get yourself a
good education, one doesn't have to drive too far across the
country to find self- validation. You will be able to validate
yourself with an education. You will know who you are and
what you are capable of doing without needing anyone else's
word but God's.

When a person is not educated, for the most part, they
become very needy because they don't know how to do anything
else. They don't know what to do or how to do it. They are just
hopeless. They find themselves always looking for someone to
validate who they are. And that is such a waste of time. Young
people, please stay in school. Don't be a dropout if you want to
be able to get a decent and productive career that you will be
proud of. I hate to be the one to tell you, but you will definitely
need a good college education in order to make that happen.
And for us older people, who have jobs that irritate the hell out
of us, please remember, it is not too late to better ourselves
and go back to school. It is never too late to change your life
for the better; you can do it, and don't let anyone tell you any
differently.

After I finished walking back and forth all day that Saturday,
late that night, the drugs began to wear off, and I began to get

sleepy. So that's when I got back in bed, curled up in a fetal position, and slept for the rest of the night up until early that Sunday morning. I got up and got some clean clothes together. I went into the bathroom and ran some nice, clean bathwater because by this time, my hygiene had gotten very foul. I could hardly stand myself. You must remember, by this time, it was Sunday morning, and I had not had a bath since early Friday morning. I was way overdue, plus I had been beaten also. My body was in trouble, big time. I wouldn't wish that on anyone. I took a good refreshing bath; I soaked in Epsom salt, baking soda, and rubbing alcohol. I sat there hugging myself and cried like a baby.

I asked myself, "How did I get to this chapter in my life? Where did I go wrong?"

People, listen to me, please stop being stupid! You got to love yourself first before anyone else can love you. It is either you do or you don't. Your actions are what make that determination. So please be mindful about how you treat yourself because people are watching you when you think they are not.

The bathroom had a big hole through the floor where termites had eaten on the property. Remember, it was just after a big rain, so it was very cold outside. Since the heating was bad inside the house, it was cold in there as well; however, that did not bother me too much. I needed that bath. So that's what I was focusing on, and I got through it by the grace of God. However, I had been through worse.

This was Sunday morning. I had to move on because the clock was ticking. It was going to be Monday morning, and Diaz would soon be in court. I had already been warned by the officers that arrested Diaz, that if I did not show up to press charges against him, a warrant would be issued for my arrest, and they would be coming after me. I had all of that on my mind. I really didn't want to go to court; like I said earlier, that was not the reason I was in Texas. All of my business had gotten twisted. Three days earlier, I was so happy, which proves that old saying: "Don't count your eggs before they hatch." My mother used to tell me long time ago when I asked her, "Mama, Mrs. McGee was not sick, but she died. Why?"

My mama said, "Baby, let me tell you something. The wellest day of your life, you are sick enough to die."

So don't get it twisted. It is what it is; bad things happen. I finally finished my much-needed bath. I went into the kitchen and prepared a meal as though it was going to be my last one. I sat at the table and ate really well. When I finished eating, I got up from the table, put my dishes away, cleaned up after myself, went into the bedroom, and laid across the bed for a little while, just thinking. My heart was heavy, and my mind was tripping. I wondered where my, and my baby's, next home would be—because I knew I was going to need one. No doubt about it. So I laid there and watched a little bit of TV. I wasn't concentrating on it, just looking at it; my mind was so far away from the TV that I really can't tell you exactly where it was. It was in so many places.

But I could not get Sweet Sadie off my mind. When I told her that I was thinking about moving to Texas with this man I had met on my job, she said, "Baby, that sounds like a mistake to me. I would not do it if I were you. You can recover from the bad choices that you have made in the past. You just got to give yourself some time. At least think about what I am saying to you before you make your move."

I said, "I will." She was a big-boned, red lady full of love for everybody. If you didn't have your head on straight, you would think Sweet Sadie was this cold-blooded woman who did not care anything about anyone but herself. However, she wasn't like that. She just would put it to you straight whether you liked it or not. She would tell you the truth about the matter, whatever it was. She would also tell you, after bursting your bubble, "You will get over it. Believe what I tell you. You'll live."

Sweet Sadie had one son, who was a wonderful young man and father and whom we knew as one of our family members even up to today—and forever. I will call him Nathanial.

As night fell, going into Monday morning, I became really depressed, especially since that was the day I was due in court to press charges on Diaz. I became very devastated and hopeless, not knowing which way to turn. I found myself in deep shit one more time. I had smoked dope with Diaz's next-door neighbor the day before; therefore, I was too ashamed to go outside the next day. So I stayed in the house all day Sunday, thinking about how I got myself into this mess and what could I do to get out of it. That Sunday night, I finally got prepared, got enough strength, and went to bed thinking really hard about what was going to happen on Monday morning.

Finally, early Monday morning came. I got up and began to gather the rest of my belongings and put them in the car that I had so regretfully purchased. I was moving around slowly, trying to make up my mind which direction that I was going to take. I definitely did not want to ask Cynthia if we could stay with her for a little while because she had her own family and problems that she was dealing with already. I did not want to put that extra strain on her because I knew she was a very nice person as it was, and I did not want to seem as though I was taking advantage of her. She did more than enough already by helping me with my baby, and today I am truly grateful for what she has done for us.

So as I continued to move around in Diaz's house, the later it got, the more worried I became. It was hell. I was still transporting my belongings from the house to the car when two of the four arresting officers showed up at the door and knocked. They asked me if I was ready to come downtown and press charges against Diaz. I really did not know what to say at that moment because I already knew that it was not my intention to press charges on Diaz in the first place. So I stood there pondering on what to say to the officers. By that time, the mail lady passed me some mail, and in that stack of mail that she gave me was the second check that I was expecting. Oh, how I jumped for joy. I knew then that everything was going to be all right.

I told those officers, "No, I was not ready to come downtown and press charges against Diaz because I am leaving for Los Angeles as soon as I can get to Cynthia's house and pick up my daughter, if you would please allow me to do so."

I was so happy that I could not wait for the policemen to leave so I could get into that car and go pick up my child, so we could be on our way back to Los Angeles.

However, the officers did warn me that without me testifying against Diaz, he would be released from jail, and we could be in danger. I said, "Thank you, officers, but now that I have the money that I have been waiting for, I will be out of Texas by nightfall."

The officers said, "Okay. We wish you well. However, just make sure you follow through with your plan."

I said, "Okay, and thank you so much." And the officers left.

After they left, I just began jumping up and down and running around the house, saying to myself, "Now I have a way out of here. I am so happy." By that time, I was all packed up and ready to go, and then the telephone rang. It was Cynthia. She asked me if I was okay. I told her, "Yes, I am doing really well, and I will be over to your house in a few minutes." I also told her that I had some good news to tell her.

She said, "Okay." I hung up the telephone. I was so very happy to be able to pay our way out of hell. I got into the car and drove over to Cynthia's house. As soon as I walked into Cynthia's house, my baby just jumped all over me, screaming, "Mommy, Mommy, where have you been? I missed you. I love you."

I said, "I missed you, and I love you too, but today we are going home, back to Los Angeles, sweetheart."

She said, "Okay, Mommy."

I gave Cynthia a big hug. She started smiling and said, "What is this all about? Tell me, I want to hear some good news too."

I said, "Oh, Cynthia, you will not believe what has just happened to me. I was standing on the front porch talking to the officers about going downtown to press charges against Diaz, which was something that I did not want to do, and all of a sudden, the mail person walked up to me and put my mail in my hand. And let me tell you what was in that stack of mail. It was the check that I had been waiting for. Now I am able to leave today for Los Angeles. If you would be so kind and take us to the bus station?"

I could see the joy in Cynthia's face. She was happy for us and for herself. I think she felt that if I could get back home, we would be all right, and the stress would be off her as well. Cynthia asked me what I wanted her to do because she would be more than happy to assist us.

I said, "Cynthia, although I purchased this car with my own money, I cannot drive it back to Los Angeles. So if you don't mind, I would appreciate if you would allow me to put all of my things into your car. And all I cannot take with me, please get rid of. Will you please do that for me? I would surely appreciate it." Cynthia said, "Oh, girl, sure, I will do that for you with no problem. Don't worry about anything because everything is going to be okay."

I said, "Cynthia, I really appreciate everything you have done for me. I will never forget how much kindness that you have shown me and my baby as long as I live, and for that, I am truly grateful. One day, hopefully, I will be able to repay you."

Cynthia said, "Oh, girl, you don't owe me anything. Just the fact that you and that baby will be safe and happy again is all the pay that I need."

Cynthia and I went outside and transported all of my things that I could bring with me on the bus from my car to her car and everything else that we could not bring with us, Cynthia and I put it on her back porch. I told her to take what she could use and throw the rest away.

After separating everything, I said to Cynthia, "Will you please take me to cash this check, and take me to Diaz's so I can leave the keys to his house and the keys to my car because I am not able to drive it back to Los Angeles, so I am just going to give it to him. From there, you can take us to the bus station, and I will pay you for doing all these things for me."

Cynthia said, "If it will make you feel any better, just put some gas in the car, and that will be all I need."

I said, "Okay, Cynthia, thank you so much."

Cynthia stopped at a red light, looked over at me, and said, "You are asking me to take you to the bus station, and from my understanding, you don't even know what time the bus leaves or what bus you will be taking."

I said, "You are so right. It doesn't matter what bus or when the bus leaves. If I have to wait two days for us to get a bus, I will because all I want right now is for me and my child to get the hell out of Texas."

Cynthia said, "I can understand that."

She took me every place I asked her to take me, but when we got to Diaz's house, he was there. I had no reason to go inside, so I asked him to come to the door, which he did. I said to him, "I am bringing you these keys today because I don't have any more use for them. You can also have the keys to the car because I am on my way back to Los Angeles. If I would have any type of car problem, I would not be able to take care of it. So you keep the car so you can have transportation back and forth to work, and I wish you well."

I walked off his front porch, and my baby waved 'bye to him. I have not seen Diaz from that day to this one, and if I would see him one thousand years from now, that would be one thousand years too damn soon.

However, about three months after leaving Texas, I called back to thank Cynthia for all she had done for us, and she said, "Geraldine, let me tell you what happened with Diaz and the car. One morning, Diaz was driving on the freeway headed to work in your car when the entire motor fell out onto the freeway. He almost lost his life. So you see, you don't have good luck when you mistreat someone just for the heck of it."

I said, "No shit."

She said, "No, I am not kidding. It really did happen. So now he is back begging for rides again. That's how it goes. It is what it is." People, people, please stop being stupid. Wake up and smell the coffee before it turns into tea. Let me tell you something. If Diaz had really wanted and loved me, I would not have had to quit my job and follow him cross-country. That was not a smart move on my part. It really was a dumb move. That's why today I will not follow a person around the corner if we cannot make it where we meet. And if that's the case, then it's so long, bye-bye.

Another thing is that, after Diaz beat me the first time, believe me, it was only going to get worse if I had stayed there in Texas. Because when a person lays hands on you for the first time, the next time, it will be easier. It does not ever get any better until one of you is dead or in jail. For the most part, it is death. Let me tell you another thing: stop being so selfish and letting it always be about "me, me, and me." What about that child whom I put through all of that mental abuse, just for the sake of a fake love affair—because there was not a damn thing about that relationship that was real. It was based on a bunch of bull crap.

When I arrived in Texas, I had cable and telephone service installed in this man's house. I put all the little womanly touches to the place. I bought a car, which was nothing to me. It was just some of the bare essentials that I felt would help make a house a home, like a chair, something that anyone else would have in their home. Evidently, Diaz did not see it like that. What he took from the situation was that I was a weak individual, needy, had low self-esteem, was looking for love in all the wrong places, acting like the boll weevil looking for a home that was not mine, and trying to make something out of nothing because everything that I just named I could have found that on my own right here in Los Angeles if it wasn't for my drug use.

All of that pain and suffering I encountered was due to my drug use, and it was no one's fault but mine. This is what you call taking responsibility for your own actions and stopping that blame game because Diaz would not have had the opportunity to beat me like he did if I had only taken responsibility for my actions and put my priorities in order, stayed in Los Angeles, continued working on my job, and left those drugs alone.

When I found out that I could not stop my drug use on my own, I should have taken it to Jesus so my prayer could get to

God the Father, and let Him know that I had a problem that I could not solve, and I needed Him to handle it for me; and just for the asking, He would have done just that. Because, people, let me tell you something, moving from state to state does not work. All those thoughts that Diaz had about me were true. I did have all those problems, and they were obvious. That's why he took advantage of me like he did. Listen, people, whenever the opposite sex connects with someone, and when they find out that person has low self- esteem; the respect for that person of low self-esteem decreases; and most of the time, that is when the abuse begins. Wake up, stop being stupid, and smell the coffee before it turns into tea because this shit is real, and it is dangerous as well. It is nothing to play with. It can and will cause a person to lose their life. I know, and I have seen it happen too many times. Your social status doesn't mean shit. If you think I am lying, listen to the news, read the newspaper. When it comes to drugs and alcohol, you are just another statistic. However, remember, this is just my truth. I am speaking only about me. If someone else can find some help in this book, just call it a blessing.

Chapter 8

Healing From Addiction through My Higher Power

Through my Higher Power, by this time, I was back in Los Angeles for approximately three months. Almost every day since I arrived, I was loaded on crack cocaine and alcohol, just completely out of my mind, drugged out. By this time, I burned my bridges; no one wanted to see me coming. I was, as far as my family and friends were concerned, nonexistent. When I would walk up to different people's doors and knock, all the lights would go out, and no one would answer. If it was in the daytime, I could hear everyone in the place saying, "Shh, shh … be quiet. Don't let her know we are in here. We don't want to be bothered with her."

That would make me feel so bad; I would just walk away and cry. People, please listen to me. When you are a drug addict of the worst kind, no one wants to be bothered with you. There are so many negative things that a drug addict carries with them. For example, for most of the time, they are not to be trusted, and they smell bad. As a matter of fact, most of us stink and don't look too good. The conversation is zero due to the fact that we can only think about one thing—where we are going to get our next hit or fix from.

People, just think about it, put yourself in the place of a clean and sober person that is trying to go somewhere in life to make something out of their lives; they don't need that negativity in their lives, and I cannot blame them. I understand that today. When I look back on my life today, there are so many regrets. Back in the day when I was loaded, I thought people were doing me wrong, but today I understand. It is a stupid mistake for anyone to try drugs of any kind because the tolerance of the first drug you try will eventually not be strong enough. And then you begin to use stronger drugs. When you start with the much stronger drug, you should already know that you are about to be in deep trouble.

People, as I said in the beginning of the book, I am not an English major. I am just putting it out there like it was put to me, straight from the shoulder. The rights of this book will never be for sale. My hope is that I want anyone and everyone to be able to read this book and understand it. That means any age. I don't want you to have to run and get a dictionary every time you read a paragraph. I want you to understand exactly what the hell I am talking about and understand that this shit is real.

So by this time, my addiction got worse. I had begun to stay with anyone who would allow me to lay my head down and rest when I had gotten too tired to stand on my own two feet. That was the type of addict I had become, one that would drink and smoke as long as there was anything in sight. If there was any way to get some dope or alcohol, I would get it; and I mean just what I said, anyway I could get it. That's how bad my addiction was.

So I continued hanging out in the streets, sleeping here and there, sleeping with whoever would allow me to sleep in their house or allow me to come in out of the rain or take a bath when I could not stand the smell any longer, or get a hot meal, which was very seldom. However seldom it was, I did not have any room to complain because I did not have anything else. At that time, I still had custody of my baby, but most of the time, she would be spending time with people like Sweet Sadie, family members, and people like that. Nevertheless, I would somehow find a way to see my baby every day to let her know how much I truly loved her. At her age, she knew in her mind that I loved her, and she knew I had a problem, but she just didn't know how to help me as much as I knew she wanted to.

Please let me tell you something. When you become a hope- to- die, out-of-control addict, it is not only about you. You hurt a lot of people like family members, friends—the few that you have left, and especially your little children. People that you don't even know care about you, you hurt as well because they know you deserve better than to die out there in the street when you really don't have to.

People, listen to me. Recovery does work, but you have to want it just as bad as you wanted that drug or alcohol. It is what you decide what your life is worth and how important you are to those who really love you; it is all about getting your priorities in order, people. So about a year after I was back in Los Angeles from Texas, I became pregnant. Although I knew the condition that my life was in, I also knew I wanted that child whom I was carrying inside of me. Abortion was not an option, as hopeless as I was. I had been through the abortion scene before, and the scar that was left on my life was unbearable. Therefore, I did not want to go through that again. With everything left in me; I knew I wanted and loved that child that I was carrying inside of me. I also knew that one day, God was going to heal me and my family.

My mother used to tell me when I was a little child that God doesn't put any more on you than what you can bear. I had been through so much by not being obedient to the way that I was raised, and what my mother used to tell me during our talks. My life had gotten so bad by not practicing what I was told as a child that I decided to resort back to my mother wit and my spirituality that I learned in my church back in Mississippi. My life was so bad at the time that I knew it could not get any worse; it had to get better. I knew about God as well. I just got on the wrong track. I always knew God was always there, but I was running on self-will; and at that time, I did not know how to stop drinking and using drugs. I was powerless. I knew what I was doing wasn't right. I knew it, but I was so taken over by the drugs and alcohol that I was out of control. I could not help myself; I was hopeless.

I tried to stop smoking during my pregnancy, but my addiction was so strong and powerful that it had taken over my life. The drugs and alcohol were making the decisions in my life. I had no control.

That's a very bad feeling to have, to let a substance take control over your life to the point that you have no say on what you do or how you do it. That is pitiful. Worse than pitiful; it is really unthinkable. Like I have been saying, if you have never tried drugs and alcohol, please don't try it because it will destroy your entire life. And those of you who are already on drugs and alcohol, there is help for you as well. It is not going to be easy; you just have to be determined.

My addiction was so powerful that I could not do it by myself. I had to put it in someone else's hands—in the hands of whom I choose to call my Higher Power, someone more powerful than myself, whom I chose to call God.

So I continued using drugs and alcohol until my due date got closer. I quit using for a couple of months; I tried to do the right thing until one night, my drug addiction overpowered me, and I took one hit off of a crack-cocaine pipe. After that first hit, I was off and running with no direction. It was not something that I had planned; it was something that just happened because I was just weak when it came to smoking crack cocaine or turning it down. I know I was supposed to say "No thanks," but when you are a full-blown crack addict, it can be very difficult to say, "I will pass this time."

After I smoked my first three hits of crack, my craving kicked in, and I wanted more. When I came to the reality that I wasn't going to be offered any more for free, I sat there in the dark and came up with a crazy solution, a wild idea of how to cop some dope on my own.

At the front door, there was a brand-new bicycle. I said, "Oh yeah, I can take that bike down the street to the dope man, pawn the bike for forty dollars' worth of crack, and go back and get it tomorrow evening." I had no way of getting that bike back, but that was what my mind was telling me. People that know what it is to have a cocaine addiction know what it is to have your mind tell you, "You don't need to pay that bill right now. Spend that money that you have on some drugs, and you will be able to get the money back for the bill later," knowing that is a big-ass lie.

I got dressed on that rainy cold night, and where I was staying; there was a very dark alley that I had to walk through to get to the dope house. I was already high from the first few hits of crack that I had just taken, so that dark alley did not faze me, not one damn bit. I was going to try and pawn that bike if there was any way possible. That bike was about to be exchanged for some crack, without a doubt. So I got the bike, walked out, and proceeded to walk the bike down to the dope house to make the exchange. On my way to the dope spot, there was a crack in the sidewalk. I had to walk the bike; I was too far gone to ride it. So I walked it—that was how determined I was to get some more dope. As I walked down that dark street, I stumbled over that crack in the sidewalk. I fell to the ground, got up, and continued to my destination.

When I got to my destination, I made the transaction that I had planned. After I completed the transaction, I returned to where I was staying. When I got back from my mission, I began to smoke that crack until I finished it. After I finished the crack and had begun to come down, some reality set in. I said, "Oh shit, what have I done?" I began to feel really strange; I had to go to the bathroom, and when I sat on the toilet seat to urinate, I looked in my underwear, and I saw some blood. I panicked. It was "a nightmare on Elm Street." You would not have wanted to be there to see my reaction. It was off the chain. I screamed, "Oh my! What have I done? I have just messed up." I ran to ask someone if they thought I would be all right, but by that time, my water broke, and I said, "I can't turn back now. It is either I go to the hospital now or give birth to my baby right here."

And that was not an option because despite everything, I still loved and wanted my baby.

It may sound stupid, but that is what crack cocaine will do to you; it will turn you into a damn fool, which is what I was at that time. This is one reason I am writing this book, to try to prevent anyone else from going through what I have gone through—being stupid and using drugs and alcohol and being out of control. If you have never used drugs and have never been an alcoholic, please don't. You will find yourself doing some things in your life that you would never think of doing if you were clean and sober.

So after reality set in that it was too late to turn back, a friend, whom I will call Daniel, drove me to the hospital. As soon as he found out that I was okay, he left. I gave birth to an eight pound baby, very healthy. After the baby was born, they took me up to a room that I shared with another young lady who had just given birth as well.

The following day, the nurse brought my roommate's baby into our room to be fed by the mother. That evening, they brought her baby back to be fed. However, I did not see my baby at all. So by this time, I began to get worried. I already knew what the problem was; I was just in denial.

I asked the nurse on the second trip, when were they going to bring my baby to me so I could feed my child. The nurse told me they were running some tests on my baby and that they thought they would have to keep my child there for a little while longer. I asked, "What is wrong with my baby?"

The nurse said, "We think your baby might be a diabetic. The glucose is a little high, but your baby is doing well. It is a very fine baby. We just need to run a few more tests. You will be able to feed your baby soon."

By this time, I was scared as hell. I was just lying there in that hospital bed thinking, *Where in the hell did I go wrong? What happened to that twenty-year-old young lady with two little children who arrived in Los Angeles with nothing on her mind but making a better life for her children and herself? What happened, and how can I fix this?*

The following day, a very nice young lady walked into the room and asked which one of us was Geraldine Thomas. I said, "I am."

And she said, "Then you are the one I am looking for." She began to tell me how beautiful my baby was. But then she told me I could not take my child home with me because there were traces of crack cocaine in the baby's system. Not much, but it was enough that I could not leave the hospital with my baby.

I said, "Please don't tell me that. I'll stop doing whatever caused this problem."

She told me that it was too late now; there was nothing else she could do for me. Then she said, "Oh, and by the way, you will be discharged today. The baby will be discharged today as well, but not to you. If you know a responsible person who will come and get the baby and keep the baby until you get some help for your addiction, that person can take the baby. You must have an addiction to smoke crack cocaine this far along in your pregnancy. All I can say is that I feel sorry for you. Please get some help, and get yourself together."

She gave me her card and said, "When you find a responsible person for the hospital to release the baby to, you contact me, and I will check with that person that you select to see if that person is a responsible source. But you only have a short time to do so because if you cannot find someone, we will."

I cried like a baby. You could hear me all the way down the hallway. However, that did not do any good. I still was discharged without my child. The only thing I could say to myself on my way out of that hospital to make myself feel a little better was "At least I did not have an abortion." At that time, I could have had one if I wanted to. They were legal. All I could think about was that one day we would be together again. So I went downstairs and visited with my baby before I left. Then I went outside where I was screaming and crying until the security guard came toward me and said, "Lady, if you don't stop all that screaming and hollering, and leave these hospital grounds right now, I will have you arrested. Haven't you done enough?"

I did not have any money to get back to where I was staying, so a lady, who was visiting the woman whom I shared the hospital room with, heard what the guard said, and she asked me, "Geraldine, would you like for us to give you a ride home?"

I said, "I would appreciate it if you would."

The lady said, "Get in. I will take you anywhere you need to go.

You will be okay."

That was another one of the worst days of my life. People, please listen to me. If you have someone in your life that loves and cares about you and your children, don't be stupid. Don't listen to your so-called friends telling you that you should leave that man, that he is too old for you, and that you should get with the drug user that is more of your style, and that you don't need that old man. The only reason they were telling me that was because they were envious of the beautiful life that I was living, and they wanted to destroy it.

But it was my fault for being stupid. I thought they meant me well until I got out there in the streets with nothing and no place to go. That's when I found out how cold, low-down, and dirty some people can be. By this time, it was too late. Someone had my man and gone. And the very ones who told me that I did not need him because he was too old were the very ones who got behind my back and said, "Geraldine sure was a damn fool to let that good man go. I wish I had him. I never would have been that stupid."

People, beware and be careful when it comes to those so-called friends because a friend is very rare. Like a jewel, a friend is very hard to find. And by chance if you are lucky enough to find one, hold on because they don't come by too often. So I rode down the street feeling really empty. I had just delivered a fine eight- pound baby and was going home alone. That was a really bad feeling, so bad it was really hard to describe. All I know is that I wouldn't wish that feeling upon my worst enemy. I finally arrived back to where I was staying and was dropped off.

I called up Sweet Sadie. I was weeping uncontrollably. She asked, "What's the matter, baby?"

I told Sweet Sadie I had just gotten discharged from the hospital after giving birth. Sweet Sadie said, "Well, congratulations. How is the baby?"

I said, "Sweet Sadie, this is the reason I am calling you. The baby is fine, but my baby was born with traces of crack cocaine in its system. The doctors would not release the baby in my care. I am calling you to ask you if you will be so kind and go to the hospital to get my baby for me, please? The Children Social Service's lady told me it had to be someone very responsible to pick my baby up in order for my baby to leave the hospital, and, Sweet Sadie, you are the only one I can think of."

Sweet Sadie said, "Sure, baby. I will go and get that baby and keep and treat that baby just like it is mine. I will keep that baby as long as necessary without a problem. When do you want me to pick the baby up? If you want me to call Mother Alice right now, let me know, and I will have her come and pick me up, and we will go and get that baby right now."

I said, "Oh, Sweet Sadie, I sure would appreciate it because the social worker told me that if I did not hurry up and get a responsible person to get the baby, they would. Sweet Sadie, I sure don't want that to happen."

Sweet Sadie said, "Give me the social worker's information and the baby's name, and I will be on my way to get the baby right now." I gave Sweet Sadie the information and said, "Thank you so much, Sweet Sadie. I will always love you for this very big deed that you are doing for me. I love you."

Sweet Sadie said, "No problem, baby. It is my pleasure to be able to help you with this very important matter. I will call you as soon as I get back. Don't worry."

I hung up the telephone and cried my heart out. Seven hours later, Sweet Sadie called me to tell me that she and Mother

Alice had made it back home with the baby, and the baby was healthy and doing very well.

Sweet Sadie said, "Mother Alice and I have just stopped off and did some shopping for the baby. Your baby has enough clothes and formula to last for at least one month, so you don't have anything to worry about because everything is going to be all right."

I said, "I will be forever indebted to you for your kindness that you have shown me today, Sweet Sadie."

But here is where another huge heartbreak came in. Mrs. Olivia, the social worker, contacted me and told me, "The baby was picked up by a very responsible person, and the baby is doing fine. But there was one very important detail that I forgot to tell you. And that is that your five-year-old has to be placed with a responsible party as well."

When she told me that, I immediately fell to my knees and screamed, "No, Mrs. Olivia, please don't ask me to give up my five- year-old. We do not have any problems. This would only destroy me."

Mrs. Olivia said to me, "Geraldine, I am very sorry that you feel this way. I am also sorry that these are the steps that we have to take. These are not my rules. It is the law. When one child is taken under these circumstances, the other children in the family have to be placed as well. The only thing I can do for you at this time is to allow you to take your five-year-old child over to Sweet Sadie's home to be with the new baby until you are able to complete the requirements in order for you to be reunited with both of your children."

Again, all I could do was cry. My heart was just torn into pieces. I called my five-year-old child, sat her down by my side, and told her, "Sweetheart, Mama needs you to do her a great big favor, and the favor is that I am not able to take care of our new baby at this time. I do not have anyone else to help Sweet Sadie with our new baby at this time. So will you please allow me to take you to Sweet Sadie's home, and you stay there with our new baby and help Sweet Sadie take care of our new baby? That way, we will make sure that everything will work out fine if you are there with our new baby."

My five-year-old said, "Mama, I don't mind helping you. But why can't you come too?"

I said, "Well, baby, at this time, I am unable to do so. But I will join you all at a later date."

My child said, "Mama, because I love you and our new baby so much, it is the only reason I am going to do this. Mama, I don't want to leave you, but I will do this for you this time. But please don't ask me to do this again because I love you."

I said, "Mama promises this will be the last time I will ask you to do a deed like this for me, sweetheart."

We spent that entire day together playing different little games, enjoying and loving each other because deep down in my heart, I knew it would be a long time before we would have this time together again. So we took well advantage of that day. People, people, please stop being stupid. Wake up and smell the coffee before it turns into tea. People, listen to me. This shit is real. The reason I went through and took my family through this misery was because I was stupid. I let drugs and alcohol get the best of me. I got my priorities twisted, and because of that, I brought a great deal of pain upon myself and others who loved me.

People, listen to me please. Drugs, alcohol, and unprotected sex are like oil and water. People, they do not mix. If you never used drugs before, don't start. Let me tell you something. If you are a real crack addict, don't let anybody lie to you. Although you know you are pregnant, as much as you know it is wrong to use drugs during pregnancy, that white devil, that crack cocaine, will overpower your pregnancy every time, and you are going to hit that damn pipe if it is any way possible.

People, one of the most shameful and disgusting acts that you ever will see is a pregnant woman smoking a crack pipe or using any type of drugs or alcohol.

While I am sitting here typing this right now, I cannot help but feel so ashamed of the activities that I participated in before and during my pregnancy. I pray that God will forgive me for all of my wrongdoing. I am so grateful that my baby is very healthy, happy, and strong today, and that is only by the grace of God.

Just a Touch Away, Right Inside of Me

The next day, I took my five-year-old child over to Sweet Sadie's home and explained to her that I was not going to be moving too far and that she would see me every day, no matter what it takes.

I walked away from my five-year-old to go to the place down the street where I was going to be staying. It was one of the hardest things I ever had to do. I walked away not wanting to, but I was court ordered.

I got down to the new place where I was going to be staying. After getting myself together and moving in, I sat down on the long brown flowered sofa, and these were the first words that came into my head, *Have you lost your rabbit-ass mind? What is it going to take to get you out of this shit?* My response to myself was *I don't have the slightest idea.*

At that moment, I was just like a brand-new baby being dropped off in the middle of the forest. I did not know what to do. All I knew was that I had messed up pretty damn bad, and it was a shame. But my next thought was *Where in the hell am I going to get my next hit from?* By that time, I was flat broke, not a dime to my name, and had no custody of either one of my small children. However, my sick mind told me, "You at least need a drink."

By this time, I was stripped. I didn't have any strings attached. I was just out there. People, let me tell you something. You don't want that. Being footloose and fancy-free, an alcoholic and a drug addict is not a good place to be in anyone's life. People, please believe what I tell you. Take it from an experienced person. Someone who has been through it, and has papers to prove it. You don't want any of that. Not everyone gets a second chance; some of us have to lose our lives in order for the rest of us to survive. About two months after my children were taken, I found myself sitting alone on the brown flowered sofa down the streets from where my children were staying with Sweet Sadie. I sat there as long as I could until I just could not take it anymore. I got up and hit the street, walking and crying. I was looking for pity, sympathy, forgiveness, understanding, a friend, a way out, even if it meant suicide. I just wanted some relief because the pain was too hard for me to bear, not realizing that everything that I was looking for was just a touch away, right inside of me— something that God had already given me for free. So I continued walking with no specific place to go, looking for something, anything that would make me feel better than I was feeling. But at that time, all I could think about was some alcohol or drugs.

As I walked down the street, before I knew it, I was at the corner, staring inside a light-colored car where this handsome young man was behind the steering wheel, staring at me and asking, "What is a nice lady like you doing out this time of the night?"

I said, "I am on my way to a place where I can find something that will change the way that I am feeling right now, for the better." I then asked the man, "Oh, and by the way, sir, what is your name, if I may ask?"

The man then said, "My name is Mr. Isadore." I then said, "What a nice name."

Mr. Isadore said, "Why, thank you. I appreciate that compliment very much."

Mr. Isadore, at that time, seemed like a very nice man. After all the hell and heart break that I had taken myself through. After all the abuse, torment, lies, backstabbing, and beatings that I had gone through. All I wanted to hear was some sweet, kind words coming from the opposite sex and Mr. Isadore gave me that. I fell for the lie one more time and again one of the biggest mistakes I ever made in my life. Mr. Isadore then said, "Will you allow me to take you to that place where I guarantee you that you will definitely feel better?"

I then said, "What plans do you have that will guarantee that you will solve this problem?"

Mr. Isadore said, "How much are you asking for to get this problem solved?"

I said, "Fifty dollars will get me started on my way to the feeling that I am looking for."

Then that's when Mr. Isadore said, "Well, that sounds like a winner to me. I don't find a problem with that. So let's go get this party started because every minute we waste will make it that much longer to get you feeling better."

I said, "Well, let's do this." I sat in Mr. Isadore's car, and he drove approximately ten miles from the location where I first met him, and parked.

I said, "Why are you stopping here? Aren't we going someplace where we will be inside?"

Mr. Isadore said, "Oh no, there is no need for that. We won't be that long."

I said, "Well, okay." By now, I began not to feel so good about this situation. At this time, the little buzz that I had was slowly leaving me. I was a little hesitant about following through with this madness. But I said to myself, *I have gone this far. I might as well go all the way now.* It was very dark where we were parked, and it was next to a railroad track. It was very frightening, but my need for my drugs, one more time, had taken priority over my fear. I prepared for Mr. Isadore to do his business. It was one of the nastiest feelings that I had ever had, but I wanted to get high so bad that I tried to put that filth out of my mind; I wouldn't wish hell like this on my worst enemies because that was exactly what it was. So after Mr. Isadore had finished his business, I got myself together as much as possible and then asked him for my fifty dollars.

Mr. Isadore gave me fifteen dollars. I said, "Oh no, Isadore, I told you fifty dollars, and you agreed." This mister shit had slipped my mind by now; now it was Isadore.

Isadore said, "I see you don't know anything about hoeing, do you? So let me give you your first few lessons. If prostitute is going to be your job title, your best bet is to get your money up front before you do anything. And second, you are to never look a gift horse in the mouth because if I gave you fifteen dollars after promising you fifty, then that means that is all I have, or that is all I am intending to give you. So what you should do is to take that fifteen dollars and get out of my car and run like hell."

I said, "Oh, hell no, you promised me fifty dollars, and that is what I want."

He said, "Okay" and ran his hand in his pocket. I just knew he was putting his hand in his pocket to get the rest of my money, but instead, his hand came out of his pocket with a large knife and stuck the tip of it in my neck and said, "Give me my motherfucking money back, and get the hell out of my car!"

I said, "Wait a minute, this was not the plan!"

He said, "Now your third lesson is, in this business, bitch, there is no plan. Everybody is different. Now get out of my car!" He then applied a little more pressure to the knife. I could feel blood dripping down my neck. He had punctured my skin.

So I said, "Okay, but how am I going to get back to where you picked me up at?"

Mr. Isadore's reply was "Bitch, you get back just like the rest of the hoes do. You walk." And then he said, "Your fourth lesson is, you are damn lucky that I didn't kill you."

So I got out of Isadore's car and started walking back toward home. All I could do was cry. I walked and cried like a baby. But by now, my feeling about the situation was *Who gives a damn about how I am feeling? My feelings are what got me into this fix in the first place. How stupid could I be?*

I could have lost my life that night just by being stupid, by putting my drug habit before my life. People, this is real. Take it from someone who knows. I cannot say this enough. If you have never used drugs and alcohol, please don't start. Crack cocaine and any drug will turn a schoolteacher into a ho. If their habit gets to the point where they feel they really need it and don't have the money to buy it, they will go to any length to get their hit or fix, and that goes for anyone, male or female, it does not matter. And those of you who are active drug users and alcoholics, there is help for you. Recovery does work, and God works even better.

My recovery came through both the program and prayer. You do whatever works for you, but what I do know is it works, so why not try it? You have tried everything else, why not try your Higher Power that I wish and choose to call my Lord and Savior, Jesus Christ. When I got out of Mr. Isadore's car, I said to myself, "Won't anyone know about this but me, Mr. Isadore, and God." Men like Mr. Isadore are what I consider damn nasty guttersnippers. My story is totally embarrassing, but God saved my life, and He saved it for a reason. So I decided that if my story, my testimony, will help save at least one person from going through all the hell that I went through, the embarrassment that I suffered was well worth it.

After about two hours of walking after getting out of Mr. Isadore's car, I finally made it back to where I was staying. When I walked in the house, there was a lady I knew. She was there waiting on me with a fifty-dollar bill for me to go and score for her. An example of how strung out I was on crack, I immediately got ready and went on another mission. I had put Isadore on the back burner and was still chasing after that white ghost. The reason they call crack the "white ghost" is, as they say, "Two is too many, and two thousand is not enough."

I continued to take the same route every day, going back and forth to the crack house to score some dope and to pass by Sweet Sadie's house where my babies were staying to say hello to them daily. I continued to get high, but I never once forgot about my babies. My addiction was so strong that it took me a little while to start working on the things that I needed to do in order to get them back into my custody.

So one day, I was on another mission, on my way to score some more drugs. As I got halfway to the spot, I happened to look across the street, and whom did I see? None other than Mr. Isadore. I stopped dead in my tracks and just stared at him. He was in the front yard of this nice house, playing ball with two small boys. I stood there for a few minutes looking at them. Mr. Isadore looked across the street to where I was standing. When he figured out who I was, he grabbed those two little boys and rushed into the house. I really didn't want any more of Mr. Isadore because he was a closed chapter in my book. So approximately three weeks later, I passed that same house where I saw Mr. Isadore and the boys playing ball in the front yard. I could see clear through that house; it was empty. Whoever lived there had moved. You go figure.

All that hell that I had gone through so far in my life was my own fault because life is about choices. You have the responsibility to try to make the right choices for your life and for your family rather than the wrong ones. Until I stopped and took responsibility for my own actions and quit that blame game, I continued to go through hell "with gasoline drawers on." I am not making light of that phrase that I just used; I really mean that.

If it doesn't look right, smell right, makes you not act right, makes you not feel right, and makes you not talk right, nine times out of ten, it is not right. People, wake up, stop being stupid, and smell the coffee before it turns into tea. Listen to me. This is real; this shit will snuff your life out like a thief in the dark. Stop playing, stop playing. This is not a joke.

You hear me quite often talk about guttersnippers, but let me make it clear. A guttersnipper is only as strong as its weakest link. Guttersnippers are always going to be out there. There is nothing we can do about that. What we can do is take control of our own lives, take back what has been stolen from us, and first of all, don't ever start with the dumb stuff. That is what will eliminate the guttersnipper's powers completely.

I had to stop that blame game and take full responsibility for all my mistakes and failures before God came in and delivered me from all that hell that I was living in. I had to surrender completely. People, you hear me speak about Mr. Isadore; however, the way I was treated by Mr. Isadore was my fault because if I had been home taking care of my family like I should have been, I never would have met Mr. Isadore. Therefore, it was my fault that I almost lost my life down by the railroad tracks.

Now all I could say to myself was "Get over it, and move on with your life because shit happens when you put yourself in certain predicaments." So I continued on my daily routine, walking in the same direction, which was leading me to nowhere but hell, to score my drugs. Day and night, it didn't make any difference as long as I got what I was going after.

Late one night, I was sitting on the sofa, listening to this minister whom I used to watch on TV on certain nights after I spent all the money that I could get my hands on to buy drugs. At the same time, I was listening to this famous radio station here in Los Angeles. I had the radio and the TV going at the same time, when suddenly, that demonic spirit came into my mind and said, *Now, damn, you don't need both the TV and the radio. You can go and trade one of them for some drugs, can't you?* I said, "Hell, yeah" one more time. How stupid could I be? Now I had started to take the things that entertained me in my home out to the dope man. I was going to trade something that gave me pleasure twenty-four seven for something that would give me a thirty-second high. That is how long it lasts. Thirty seconds, and it is over.

It doesn't ever get any better. It only gets worse. As long as I was in denial, I always stayed in pain.

So that night, I followed my first mind, and the item that I decided that I did not need was the nice-looking medium-sized yellow radio that got all the stations. Something that was very dear to me, but my drug addiction took priority over what was dear to me. Like always, I felt at that time that I needed the drugs more than I needed the radio. So I snatched the cord out of the wall socket. And what was so cold about it was that I had just put new batteries in it the day before so I could sit out on the front porch to listen to it in my slow moments. That radio was really nice. It could operate with batteries or electricity. Now how cool could that be?

So I headed out on my mission to trade the nice little yellow radio that was very dear to me for some crack cocaine because I really was spooked, sprung, and sparked. It was a bad feeling, and I did not want to keep that feeling because more than thirty seconds had passed, and that last hit was way out in the ozone someplace. There was no way I could get that one back. That was a done deal. Therefore, I had to find another option. All the money was gone, so the only thing I could see at the time was the radio that I had in my hands. And I was on my way to the dope spot, trying to satisfy my craving.

People, let me be clear when you hear me speak about the dope spot; I am speaking of any spot on the streets wherever they were standing outside selling crack cocaine. I was never big enough to have an address to cop from or names, only the streets understood. Therefore, I would walk until I could find someone standing on the streets selling crack. That's how I got taken so many times. When I say *taken*, I mean I have purchased plain rocks that someone had picked up off the ground and wrapped in foil. I have also purchased nice-size pieces of soap that you bath with wrapped in foil. There are all types of games people play in this field, and there is no use in going back talking about "Man, this is soap" or "This is a rock off the ground that you just sold me" because that person is long gone— gone somewhere smoking using the same money that they have just gotten from you. Now, one more time, how stupid could I be? In this game, one will find themselves saying this quite often. So the best thing to do is *don't start it*. I cannot say this enough.

So as I walked the streets with the little radio, I got about three miles from the house, and I looked over to my left. As I stood on that lonesome corner waiting for the traffic light to change, I saw this lighter flick in the dark, in this large, vacant fenced-in field that was filled with tall grass. I recognized that flick from far across the streets. That is how strung out I was. One thing for sure, one drug addict knows another, and you can take this to the bank. That is how real this shit is. So as I walked past the vacant field, the young man inside of the fence said, "Hey, lady, where are you on your way to this late at night?"

I replied, "I am on my way to see if someone wants to make a trade."

The young man said, "What do you have to trade?"

I said, "A portable radio."

He said, "I might want to make that trade because that is what I am doing right now, smoking crack." I said, "Really."

He said, "Yes, and by the way, I forgot to tell you, the music is really sounding good." I said, "No shit."

He said, "That's right! Why don't you climb on over this fence and let us see what we can come up with."

I said, "I see you around here all the time. What is your name?" He said, "My name is Willard. What's yours?"

I said, "My name is Geraldine. I figured as often as I have seen you around here, I thought you knew my name."

He said, "No, I have seen you many times, but I never knew your name."

I said, "Well, you know it now, and if you are interested in this radio, let's get started with the business. Enough of the small talk." So I passed Willard the radio, and I hopped over the fence. By the time I hopped over the fence of that vacant lot, Willard's whole demeanor had changed just that quickly.

Willard said, "Let's see what this damn thing can do." When he said that, I immediately got nervous. I said to myself, "I have just fucked up."

By this time, Willard grabbed my collar with both hands and threw me to the ground. Then he whistled, and this very large dog came running up to me. The big black dog got right in my face and started growling very loudly. Every now and then, it would bark.

Willard said, "If you don't do what I tell you, I will have my dog eat your face off."

I said, "Willard, please don't hurt me. Please don't let your dog bite me. Please don't!"

Willard said, "Take your pants down right now, bitch. Who do you think you are to tell me let's get down to business? I am going to show you what business that I am interested in."

By now, I was crying uncontrollably. I was scared to death. I said, "Willard, if you love yourself and your dog, you will take the radio and let me go. You can have the radio. I don't want anything for it. It is yours!" I continued, "Willard, I have a very serious problem. If you allow your dog to bite me, he will get infected and die. Please don't let this happen to your dog. Willard, if you allow any of my blood to get on you or your dog, you both will die. That is just how infected I am. Please, let me go, and you can keep the radio. I will never tell anyone about this night. I promise!"

Willard said, "Bitch, are you lying?"

I said, "No, I am not lying. I am telling you the truth. Please, believe me."

Willard said, "You better not be lying, and you better not tell no one about this. Do you understand me?"

I said, "Yes, I understand you."

Willard said, "Now you can go, but this damn radio is mine, and don't you come back."

Willard said something to that dog, and it moved back so I could get up. When the dog moved back, I jumped over the fence and ran like hell and never looked back. I ran all the way home. When I got in the house, I was out of breath, but one more time, I barely escaped with my life.

Although I lied about the fact that I had a serious blood disease, I did not feel bad about it because that was the only solid thing I could come up with at that time that might save my life. Willard didn't have any plans on allowing me to leave that vacant lot without being harmed or killed. My gut feeling tells me if I hadn't told that lie about a blood disease, I would be dead today.

This shit is real. It is not worth the chances that we take just to get a thirty-second high. That's all it is, chasing that white ghost, something that we will never catch up to no matter how fast we run. Like the old saying goes, "Two is too many, and two thousand is not enough." If you are not a drug addict or alcoholic, please don't start because there is nothing good that will come out of being a sick and hopeless addict. And for those of you that are abusing drugs already, I just stopped by today to let you know that recovery does work, and what I am triple sure of is, I know for a fact, that prayer definitely works. That's what did it for me. That is how I got healed—through prayer and what my Higher Power did for me. I truly believe he will do it for you, free of charge.

So I continued to walk the streets back and forth, searching for that imaginary high that I was not going to get. But at that time, I did not know I was chasing that white ghost, something that was never going to materialize. So I just kept on beating those streets and kicking rocks with no direction, just insane, hopeless. That continued for a few years, back and forth, day and night, right or wrong, with or without, it did not matter as long as I had the smallest hope that I was going to get some drugs, even if it was just a small hit of crack. I kept right on walking with no place to go.

So after about two years, I got pregnant one more time. That kind of slowed me down a little bit, but not much. I was still beating the streets and acting like a plain fool. I would not listen to any logic, only nonsense. How stupid could I be? People, people, listen to me. If you are one of those party people, and you get pregnant, common sense should tell you that it is time to go somewhere and sit down and stop that insane shit.

So I continued on until I gave birth to a fine baby. After the baby was born, I continued to get high, just out of control— until one night. I had stayed up all night long. Matter of fact, I had been up for a few days, and I was bone tired. I locked up all the doors and lay down beside my baby with my arm across my child, thinking everything would be okay. But again, things did not go as planned.

I was awakened by my landlord. May God rest her soul. With her, there were two policemen who were holding my baby's hands. They asked me what happened. I responded by saying, "Oh, there is no problem here, officer! We are okay. What is the matter, officer? Is there something wrong that I don't know about?"

The officer replied, "Yes, there is a problem. We were called out here by your landlord. She stated in her call that your baby was walking around outside partially dressed and unattended. What is your answer to that? Because that is definitely how we found your child."

I replied by saying, "Mrs. Naomi, you didn't call the policeman on me and the baby did you? All you had to do was come and knock on the door and wake me up. I live right down the hall from you. You have a key to my apartment. You did not have to do that. Did you really do that, Mrs. Naomi?" I then said, "Officer, I don't doubt what you say. I just want to hear Mrs. Naomi tell me she really did this to us."

Mrs. Naomi replied by saying, "Yes, I called them. And if necessary, I would do it again."

I was knocked off my feet. I was blown away. I just could not believe that woman could stoop that low after speaking to me and my child each and every day as we passed her place. I just could not believe it. But by her telling me to my face that she made that call, I had no other choice but to believe her. By now, Mrs. Naomi was irrelevant. I was through talking to her for the moment. I had to put my focus back on the officers in order to find out where my child and I stood, and try to do some damage control because by now, I was up shit's creek without a paddle. So I said to the officers, "Can we just fix this right here, right now? I will give you my word that this will never happen again in life."

The officers said, "Ms. Thomas, we cannot leave this child here in your custody. This child could have gotten seriously hurt by being outside unattended. And your neglectful behavior is inexcusable. Therefore, you should be happy that we are not taking you to jail for child endangerment. This child will be taken from you and put in protective custody, and you will be notified at a later date where this child is being kept."

I then said, "Wait a minute, officer. Please listen to me for a few seconds, please?" I went on to say, "I already have two children around the corner with my aunt. Her name is Sweet Sadie. She will take my baby until I can get things straightened out. Will you please do this for me and not take my child to some strange place?"

The officer replied by saying, "We are aware of the fact that you have two other children around the corner. Mrs. Naomi has informed us of that already."

I said, "Here is her address and her telephone number. Please try this first?"

The officer then said, "We have to check back in with headquarters. If this is okay, you will be notified. In approximately one hour, contact your aunt and see if your child is there. We cannot make any promises at this time."

I thanked the officers. The officer said to me, "In the meantime, Ms. Thomas, try and get yourself together. You and your children deserve better than this. You can do it if you really want to. Follow through with the plan that the courts have assigned to you, and you and your family will be all right."

I said, "Thank you all so much. I am definitely going to do that. Thank you."

Mrs. Naomi was standing at my front door, looking at me with a smile on her face. She was hoping that they would have taken me to jail; that was her plan. Mrs. Naomi was a big-boned woman with light-brown skin and long wavy hair, very shapely, but had a heart made out of ice—a cold-blooded sister; in my terms, a *guttersnipper*. After all that, I was still thankful that things turned out as well as they did because my baby did not get hurt, and my baby was also taken right to Sweet Sadie to be with siblings. I called Sweet Sadie about one hour after the officers had left with my child, and she told me, "Yes, Geraldine, I have the baby. Don't you worry. I will keep this child as long as necessary. Just work on getting yourself together, and I will handle this end."

I said, "Thank you so much, Sweet Sadie. As long as I live, I will never forget you or Nathanial for opening up your door and your heart to us. Thank you, thank you."

What Mrs. Naomi did to harm, God turned it around for the good. She really did me a favor. I don't think she was ever able to realize what an impact that telephone call to the policemen had on my life. I don't think she ever realized it. People, people, please listen to me. Wake up and smell the coffee before it turns into tea, and stop being stupid because this shit is real. Not only can you lose your life dealing with drugs, but you can also lose your loved ones' lives as well.

Mrs. Naomi called the policemen on me, and I was very, very angry with her for a very long time. I had to stop and think about what part I played in Mrs. Naomi calling the cops on me. After looking at the situation long and hard, I concluded that all the problems that I was having in the past, present, and future started with me. Until I quit that blame game, stood up on my own two feet that God had given me, and stopped singing that old song about "poor me, poor me," I realized that I was never going to recover or be healed.

"Recovery starts with you taking an inventory of your life."

When I stopped all that nonsense and took full responsibility for all the things that had happened to me in my life, that's when, and only when, God would come into my life and allow me to recover and be healed from all of that insanity. People, He will do it for you as well. For you nonbelievers, being healed from drugs and alcohol and getting recovery, it does exist, it is real, and it can happen. It is possible for you to live a sober life as well as anyone else. People, you have the right as much as anyone else to live a clean and sober life for yourself and your loved ones. It starts with you taking inventory of how and when you reached this point in your life where you had no more control over how you lived your life and what should be done to repair it.

When my last baby was taken from me, which was the straw that broke the camel's back, I started thinking. Although I wasn't completely healed, or recovered, at that time, I started thinking and trying to put my priorities in order.

After I allowed my last child to be taken from me, something changed in my soul. It seemed as if I had been violated to the third degree one more time, but as I said earlier, I was not quite healed as yet. I still had a long way to go. I cannot tell you all that happened to me in those twenty-five years that I am speaking of, but I am going tell you more about the changes that drugs and alcohol took me through, and what a profound impact it had on my life.

As you read through my book, you will be able to recognize that I am not an English major, but what you will find in here is that I do have is a PhD from "Street University." An education that I would not recommend to anyone. It is too painful. One thing you will find out about Street University is that you will pay a high cost for low living. And, people, it is not worth it. There is some embarrassing information that I am writing about in this book, but God saved my life. And I thank God for Jesus because the only way you can get through to the Father is through Jesus Christ, or to whomever you decide to call your Higher Power. I choose God the Father, the Son, and the Holy Ghost. Because God was so good to me that I feel compelled to tell somebody, anybody, and everybody about how good God is. That is the least I can do considering what He did for me. People, people, please wake up and smell the coffee before it turns into tea because this shit is real. "Street University" will kill you if you allow it to do so. But what I stopped by here to tell you today is that recovery and deliverance is possible. Recovery works! God is in the deliverance business, and you can have both just for the asking.

People, drugs are killing too many of our people of all avenues. I am speaking of pharmaceutical drugs as well as crack and other drugs. A drug that has been issued through a pharmacy can be as deadly as drugs that you get from the streets, if they are not used as directed. If you think I am lying, read the newspapers, watch TV, log on to the Internet, and other sources of the news. You will see that these drugs are taking our people out in big numbers. And one thing about drugs is that they don't give a damn about who you are or what your background is. If you get caught slipping, you will become another statistic just like the rest of us. Now go figure.

By now, all my children were in the custody of Sweet Sadie until I could get my act in order; which seemed as though it was so very hard to do. I can remember crying many nights during that time. I finally realized that crying was not going to take care of the problem. I had to do a lot more than shed tears. I knew I had to clean up my life in order to even be considered for getting my children back. But I continued on smoking crack. Now I was alone and had no one to hide from anymore. Now my crack smoking and alcohol drinking was between God, the crack man, the liquor stores, and me. What a lonely life to live. So I continued to get high, trying to cover up the hurt, pain, and shame that I was going through.

One night, I had spent all my money. Now the cookie jar was empty. I had no more change in the cookie jar. So I came up with this wild idea to go out in the streets to see if I could find someone that wanted to spend some money on me. By now, I was sitting there alone, and it seemed as though the walls were just closing in on me to the point that I just could not take it any longer. I had to do something to get high, even if it was wrong. That's exactly the way I was feeling. So I got my clothes together, went into the bathroom, took a bath, cleaned myself up, got dressed, and walked out the door as if I was going to a legit job and I could give a damn about whom I was going to meet out there. It really didn't matter. I was ready for anything that came my way. So I walked to the first corner and stopped dead in my tracks, as if this was the spot I was supposed to be in. I had no idea that I would stop right there on that particular corner when I left my house, but I did. I just stopped there and waited—for what, I had no idea. I just stood there like a silly little fool, messed up inside. In about ten minutes after stopping on that corner, this sharp-ass Beamer pulled up. Inside of it was this nice, soft-spoken, wavy-haired, brown-skinned, handsome young man in a double-breasted suit. He pulled into the service station where I was, pulled up right close to where I was standing, and said, "Hello, miss, what's a nice young lady like you doing out this time of night?"

I said, "I am trying to make it happen." He said, "What is your name?"

I said, "Geraldine."

He said, "Nice name. It fits you."

I said, "Thank you, and what's your name?"

He said, "My name is Freddie. How do you feel about allowing me the opportunity to help you make it happen?" He opened the car door for me from the inside, and I got in. We drove around the corner, and he parked the car. He said, "What do you need to make it happen for you?"

I told him I needed fifty dollars. Freddie said, "That is something I can handle without any problem."

I said, "Well, let's get active, then."

Freddie had the patience that you would not believe. He politely took his jacket off and laid it on the back seat. Then he unfastened his vest and laid it on top of his jacket. And lastly, he loosened his tie, removed it from his shirt collar, and laid it on top of his vest. Freddie was so articulate that I just enjoyed talking to him as well as watching him. Freddie then reclined the seat, and we took care of what we had to do. After it was over, I was ready to hop out of the car and go make it happen for me, until Freddie said, "Can we talk for a few minutes?"

I said, "Yes, if you have the time."

He said, "Time is not an issue for me. I want to talk to you about your happiness, if you don't mind." I was a little thrown off by his concern. He said, "Do you have any children?"

I said, "Yes."

He asked, "Do you have custody of them?"

I said, "No, they are with my aunt, who lives right around the corner."

He asked, "Do you see them?" I said, "Yes, every day."

Freddie said, "Will you promise me a few things, Geraldine? Promise me that you will try and get back with your children because they deserve to have you in their lives as much as you deserve to have them in your life. Geraldine, will you also promise me that after you finish doing what you wanted to make happen, please go home, and don't come back outside tonight. It is too cold for you to be out in this type of weather."

I said, "Thank you, Freddie, for your concern. It means a lot to me, more than you will ever know."

During this entire conversation, the car seat was still in a reclined position, and I was lying there with my head on his chest. The fragrance that Freddie was wearing was awesome. Fourteen years later, I can still recall it in my low moments, or when I want to feel the safety net that I felt that night. We must have talked lying there for at least twenty minutes, and they were twenty minutes that I will cherish for the rest of my life. I got so comfortable lying there with Freddie I found myself sort of dozing off. That's how comfortable I had gotten with Freddie until, all of a sudden, I gathered myself, I sat up, and I said, "Freddie, is that all you want me to promise you?"

He said, "Yes, for the moment."

I was so taken by his kindness, but I said, "Okay, Freddie, I won't hold you any longer."

He said, "You are not holding me. I am enjoying you as much as I feel you are enjoying me."

I said, "Okay, but I got to go now." I knew he had something that I wanted to last, but due to my circumstances, I knew it was not possible. I was so amazed by how we connected that I got out of Freddie's car and left the money. I got to the back end of his car when he tapped his horn lightly. I went back to the car, and there was Freddie saying, "You forgot something," and he passed me three twenty-dollar bills.

I said, "Oh, yes, Freddie, I didn't, I—"

He said, "I wasn't about to let you do that. Oh, yes, Geraldine, there is a man somewhere for you that will really love you and give you the things you and your children need. Please don't give up."

I said, "I won't, Freddie. I'll see you around."

When I walked away, I was in a daze. Like what in the hell just happened? Was this an angel or what? When I continued to walk away from Freddie's car, I gave him a new name, one that I will forever remember him by, and that name is Fabulous Freddie. Somehow, I feel Freddie was somebody's husband because that package was too perfect and too well wrapped to be single. Freddie motivated me to get my life together. There was something about him that stuck in my mind even to this day. I will never forget about him, and there is a part of me that doesn't want to forget about him. It has been fourteen years since I saw Fabulous Freddie. I just want to say, Freddie, thank you. You know who you are.

Chapter 9

I Can Smile Today, and It Is Not Fake

After I left Freddie, I went straight to the liquor store and bought whiskey, beer, and cigarettes. From there, I went to the dope spot and scored some crack. And from there, I went home and laid my spread out. I had crack, liquor, cigarettes, beer, and pills. I also had three Bibles open, which I kept open all the time, regardless, because I knew the way I was living wasn't right, and I needed some help. Not only was it not right for me, it was not right for my children either.

Listen to me, people. We have to stop jumping in these cars when we don't know who these people are. I was just lucky that Freddie was a nice man. It is very rare that we meet people like Freddie. The majority of the time, when we meet people in circumstances like I met Freddie, for the most part, my life would have been in danger like many times before. Not only did I feel Freddie was someone's husband, I also felt that he was someone's father; he left that impression on me. As I sat there with all those different types of drugs and alcohol in front of me at my home, I was also listening to this black minister who would come on TV and spread the word about the goodness of the Lord. The message was something that I really needed to hear. I was sitting with two glass pipes so I would not let one pipe cool before I hit the crack again. It was ridiculous that I had so many different types of drugs sitting on one table in front of one person—me. All of a sudden, I felt a full hand covering the top of my head. I thought it was the young man that I was living with at that time. But when I turned around to tell him to stop playing, I discovered that no one was in the room but me. I know I felt that whole hand on the top of my head without a doubt.

I sat there and thought about the way my life was going, how my children's lives were going, and the talk that I had just had with Fabulous Freddie, and I just broke down and started crying like a baby. I could not hold it in any longer. I knew that hand I felt was God's hand. That is when I knew that my life was about to take a turn for the better.

I still did not know exactly what was going to happen because at that moment, I was still addicted. But I knew a change was about to come. When or where, I did not know. All I knew was that I felt different, to the point that all the drugs and alcohol that I had in front of me to get high on, somehow, the value of those things had depreciated. That's when I began to cry out louder and louder to the Lord. I knew a change had to take place because I could not live like that too much longer. The weight had gotten too heavy and too much for me to bear.

My Deliverance Prayer

Dear Lord, I come to you with a humble heart and a bowed down head. Lord, I am coming to you, asking you to please forgive me for all of my sins. Lord, I need you to deliver me from the way I have been living because I cannot do it all by myself. I have tried and I have failed. My way is not working. Father, I need you to come in and take control of my life, and teach me how to live again. Lord, I have been beaten all of my life in some type of way. Lord, I have been beaten out of my homes, out of my cars, out of my dignity, out of my furniture, out of my jobs. But most of all, Lord, I have been beaten out of my little children's lives. If there is any way a person can be beaten, Father, I have. Lord, I thank you for sparing my life. I know it's only by your grace and mercy that I still stand. In spite of everything that I have been through, Father, I still honor and praise your name. You are the best blessing that I ever received. Without you, there would be no me. This I do know.

Lord, I am tired of living the way that I have been living. I have no place else to turn; I am at my bottom. I pray that you will have mercy upon my soul, Father, and reunite me with my little children so I will be able to raise them to be good people, good citizens, like my parents raised me to be. I want my mind back, Lord, because right now, I am not in my right mind. Drugs and alcohol have taken over my thinking and decision making. I want back what Satan, drugs, alcohol, and the streets have taken from me. Father, you said, "Ask and I shall receive." I do believe you are going to deliver me and heal my body. I believe it. I truly believe it because, Father, I have gone as far as I can go. I cannot make it any further without you intervening in my whole situation, taking control of my entire life, and showing me how to live again. Father, I am not asking for justice, I am asking for mercy because I am so tired. I have the faith, Father. I do have the faith. And most of all, I thank you for Jesus. Lord, I thank you for all of those many wonderful things that you have done for me in my life. I do not want to seem ungrateful because you have been so good to me in spite of me, in spite of everything that I have been through, and for that I am truly grateful.

Lord, I thank you for all that you have done for my little children, sparing their lives, keeping them healthy and happy. Thank you, Father, for everything. Lord, I thank you for taking care of everyone, even people that I don't even know. Amen.

I revealed all of these degrading things about myself to make a point. And that point is, no matter what we have done in our lives, God will forgive us. My Higher Power that I choose to call God the Father, the Son, and the Holy Ghost, is always in the forgiveness and miracle-working business. I stopped by today to let you know that God did not create us to be drug addicts, alcoholics, prostitutes, criminals, repeated offenders, or murderers. That was not God's plan for our lives. It is a long ways from it.

People, it is never too late to change your way of living. Living recklessly is not of God because God is not about confusion. The way I was living was nothing but confusion. And because God looked beyond my faults and saw my needs, today I am truly, truly grateful. So after I found myself alone in a dark room one more time, and after feeling that invisible hand on top of my head, I still hadn't quite gotten it. So I continued on getting high for a few more days. A few days after meeting Fabulous Freddie, I was walking with a lady, whom we will call Jennifer, on my way to borrow some money when this black-and-white Cadillac drove by, and the driver blew the horn. I looked at Jennifer, and she looked at me. I said, "Do you know who that is in that car?"

She said, "No, do you?" I said, "No."

So we just brushed it off and continued on walking. A few minutes later, that same car pulled up where we were, and that was when I discovered who was in the car. It was Mr. Jam. I was very shocked to see him, but happy at the same time. He got out of his car, walked toward me, and said, "This nonsense that you are doing to yourself and your little children has gone on far too long. It is time for you to make a change. You cannot continue like this too much longer. You don't know this, but I have been keeping up with you. And actually I was driving down this street today looking for you to tell you if you go and get yourself some help, I will stand by you as long as you need me to. You will never want for anything. I'll always be there for you. But you must go into an in-house program because you look really bad."

I agreed. So he said, "You know the telephone number. After all these years, it is still the same. When you get in the program, call me, and I will be there."

I said, "Okay, Jam."

So I got the money from Jennifer, but I could not bring myself to go to the spot and cop some crack. So I went next door to the liquor store, bought some beer and cigarettes, and went back to Jennifer's house. She had gone on ahead of me. When I got back to her house, she said, "You are back already?"

I said, "Yes, I only went to the store. I could not bring myself to go anyplace else."

She said, "Well, that's good."

After drinking some of that beer that I had bought, I curled up on her floor in a fetal position and attempted to go to sleep, still thinking about the talk that I had just had with Mr. Jam. Jennifer worked at night, so on her way out to work, she stopped and said, "Geraldine, you cannot continue to go on like this. You must get some help."

I said, "Okay, Jennifer. When you get home in the morning, I will be gone. And by the way, thanks for everything."

She said, "You are welcome! I wish you well."

She went on to work. About five o'clock the next morning, I called Edward. Edward was a man that I met through the young man that I was living with. Edward had told me that when I was ready to clean up my life, to call him, and he would give me a ride to a recovery home at no cost. I always remembered Edward's number. So that very next morning, I called Edward and told him that I was ready to go and get some help. I told him where I was. Edward said I will be right there. I said OK Edward and hang up the telephone. I was at my bottom, I had no place to go, and I lay there on that floor and began to talk to myself. I asked myself, "Whatever happened to that lady that came to California from Mississippi in search of a better life for her and her little children? What happened? Where did I go wrong? How did I end up on this lady's floor with no place to go?"

After that monologue, I broke down crying again and couldn't stop. At that moment, Edward was knocking at the door. I went to the door and there he stood, asking me, "Are you ready to go Geraldine?"

I said, "Yes, this is it. It is over. Let's roll."

I gathered the few belongings that I had left, went out, gotinto the truck, and we drove away. When we got about a mile from the recovery home, I said to Edward, "When we get to the next liquor store, stop."

Edward said, "Stop for what?"

I said, "I am going to buy me two more cans of beer." He said, "Why?"

I said, "Because I want to say good-bye to the drugs and alcohol." I could tell he wasn't pleased with my request, but he said, "Okay, Geraldine, but make this your last stop that we make before

we get to that recovery home."

I said, "Okay, Edward." He stopped. I ran into the store and bought two cans of beer, and I got back into the truck. I finished both cans in about fifteen minutes, got rid of the cans, and said, "Good-bye to drugs and alcohol."

About a month after I was in the recovery home, I called Mr. Jam and told him where I was. He stayed right by my side until God called him home in 2004. For the love that he showed my family and me, I will never forget him as long as I live. I consider Mr. Jam a true friend. That is why I say that if you ever get one, you hold on for dear life because they are like a jewel, very few and very rare.

About six weeks after I was in the recovery home, one night, the ladies and I were in Bible study. We were discussing certain chapters in the Bible, and all of a sudden, this thought came. I asked the ladies if they would join me in a circle of prayer. I was still smoking cigarettes, but I did not want to continue doing so. So I asked for the circle of prayer, and the ladies agreed. I started praying out loud, asking God to keep me because I did not want to go back to the type of life that I had been leading. I prayed so hard that night until the walls came down. During the time I was praying, I felt a warm glow come all over my body. When Bible study was over, I felt different, better, and I have not smoked another cigarette since that night. I know it was only by the grace of God that I haven't had any crack, and I haven't had the urge to use. It is not a struggle for me today—to God be the glory.

I stayed in recovery for one year. When I completed the program, I was blessed with a nice place to live at this sober living home where this wonderful lady helped me to get my children back. I will call her Mrs. Ann. Today, she is still a friend of mine. Those of you who contributed to my recovery, I would like to take this time out now to say *thank you*. You know who you are. Thank you again.

Anything and everything that my Higher Power did for me, I truly believe that He will do it for you. Just try Him. What do you have to lose? God is not through with me yet. I am still a work in progress. I may not be what I want to be, but I sure am not what I used to be. And for that, I am truly grateful. Today, I am living in South Central with my family. I am not saying everything is going smoothly because it is not. I still have my problems, but I have not found any reason to pick up a drink or use drugs. I know it is not of my doing; I cannot take any credit for my sobriety or my life today. Again, I cannot say it enough, that it is only by the grace of God and His mercy that I am alive today. I am happy, I am sober, I can smile today, and it is not fake.

In my sobriety, I am furthering my education. As of now, I have received two college degrees and a certificate. My goal is to obtain a master's degree in psychology, and with God's help, I wll get there, I pray. One of the best decisions that I ever made in my life was to further my education. To God be theglory.

Thank God for Jesus!

Chapter 10

❧

My Bottom

I know after you read this book, you must be asking yourself, "Well, what was Geraldine's bottom?" Well, I am going to tell you, although at one time, I said no one would ever know about this night but me and God. But I feel that if I am going to tell my story, I might as well tell exactly what I know was my bottom back in 1996. One weekend toward the end of my addiction, I had been on a three-day binge with little to no sleep after receiving an amount of money totaling approximately two thousand dollars. I went crack- cocaine-buying crazy. I had smoked so much crack cocaine until it seemed as though the more I smoked, the sober I became; I had no self-control. I spent down to my last sixty dollars, and that's when reality began to set in. The reality check was that I spent all my money, and I still wasn't high. What was the point? After that reality check, it seemed as if every nerve in my body started shaking, not quivering. I mean just what I said, shaking.

I had spent all that money and hadn't bought myself as much as a ninety-nine-cent pair of earrings. Now I was totally depressed, so I decided to go across the track and buy another fifty-dollar rock, hoping that would make me feel better about myself and I would get rid of the shakes. When I got over to the spot where I could score a fifty-dollar rock, I met with the guy and told him I wanted to score some smoke. He said, "How much?"

I said, "Fifty dollars' worth."

He said, "Well, Geraldine, you have been spending with me all weekend. I just finished cutting it up. If you will take these crumbs off my hand with this buy, I will fix you up real good."

I said, "Okay."

That is what you call falling for the dumb stuff. So then the guy poured the crack crumbs in my hand, they were not wrapped in anything—no foil, no Saran Wrap, no nothing. It came right out of the plate into my hand. People, let me tell you one thing. To show how addicted I was to crack, when that crack touched my bare skin, my stomach immediately reacted to it; my stomach just started flipping, turning over and over, and at that time, I had an instant BM to the point I could not control it. I paid the guy and started walking back home, and it seemed as though every ten steps that I would make, I would have another BM to the point that when I made it to the place where I was living, I was in a bad condition. But what made me really realize that I had reached my bottom was, when I made it home with the crack cocaine crumbs in my hands, I was so anxious to get inside the house and smoke that when I did get the door unlocked, I went straight to the back room at the end of the hallway, put the crack on the plate, and stood there and smoked for approximately two hours until all the crack was gone—without ever changing my clothes. The stench that was in that hallway was so bad that if someone who was in their right mind would have stopped by, they would not have been able to stand it. It was just that bad. After I finished, I got out of those clothes. I took a bath. After the bath, I took the clothes out to the trash can, and I came back into the house, and that was when reality began to set in. I said, "I have spent approximately two thousand dollars, and I don't have a damn thing to show for it. All I got out of this was a very low and degrading way of living for a high cost."

For me, at that time in my life, two thousand dollars was a lot of money for a poor struggling drug addict like I was. I went in the bathroom and looked in the mirror for the first time in a long time, and what I saw scared me to death. I looked so bad. When I did brush my teeth, I would always look down. I never would look in the mirror until that one night that I am speaking about now. When I looked into that mirror in my bathroom, I screamed at the top of my lungs, and that was when I said, "Oh my God, what in the hell has happened to me? How did I get to this point in my life?"

That was when I said, "If there was ever a bottom to reach, then I have arrived."

I started weeping uncontrollably to the point I could not stop. I cried for hours until I cried myself to sleep right there in the middle of that floor where I had fallen and curled up in a fetal position. All I could think about was where were my little children, and how did I let this happen to us. When did this start? I did not know it would come to this, I just did not know. People, people, please stop being stupid, and wake up and smell the coffee before it turns into tea. Drugs and alcohol will destroy you. If you have never used drugs and alcohol, people, please don't. Take it from a person like me who has already been there and done that. I almost lost my life behind it. Please listen. Those of you who have already started, I stopped by today to let you know that recovery does work, and God works even better. I had bottomed out to the point I stopped asking for recovery. I started asking God for a healing. I told God,

"Father, if you will heal my body and my mind from this evil substance, I give you my word that you will never have another problem out of me using crack ever again." I meant that then, and I mean it up until this day.

People, people, please listen. For many years, I said that no one would ever know about my stories that I have told in this book but me and God, but I have been thinking about how good God has been to me and my family to the point that I said I got to tell somebody about His mercy and grace that He had shown me. If it was not for God's mercy and grace, I would be dead, and I know this. It would be wrong if I kept these blessings to myself and not let someone else know what God did for me. He will do it for you if you just ask. It took me many years before I could open up and make up my mind to tell about God's goodness, how He healed my body and mind from crack cocaine. But I also remembered that it is written that "If you deny Me before your friends, I will deny you before My Father,"and the Lord knows I cannot afford that. You know, people, I thought about how I had to get comfortable in my own skin before I could come out and tell about the time that I lost control of my body functions and the terrible smell I encountered.

I began to think about how we have lost millions of our sisters and brothers to this terrible disease called drug addiction.They were decent people who could have had a very bright future if they hadn't gotten caught up in the drug scene. I feel someone has to speak out about this terrible disease and to tell the truth, the whole truth. So I decided it might as well be me, along with other information that is out there. This shit needs to be voiced out all over the world because this is where it is happening—all over the world. Drugs and alcohol do not discriminate. If you think I am lying, think back a few years and count some of our people that this evil substance has taken out. And don't get it twisted; when I say my sisters and brothers, I am speaking of all nationalities, not one race, but all.

This addiction doesn't care who you are, how much money you have, or what background you come from. If you leave yourself open by making the wrong choice, it will grab a hold of you and run like hell, and when you wake up one day, it is twenty-five years later. People, I don't want to see this happen to you because if you fool around and make the wrong choice, it will happen. People, people, please wake up and stop being stupid. Addiction will kill you, and it won't look back. This shit is real; it is no joke. If you have never tried crack cocaine, please don't get started. If you are addicted already, know that recovery does work, and God works even better. The way I got through twenty-five years of drug and alcohol addiction was with prayer, and I do believe your Higher Power will do the same thing for you. God healed my body and mind to the point that even after twenty-five years of a long hard addiction, I don't even think about using illicit drugs at all today. I also prayed to God to deliver me from smoking two packs of cigarettes a day for approximately thirty years, and He did. I have not smoked crack or cigarettes in twenty years, and I know this is only because of God's mercy and grace that I am able to say this and mean it—and for this, I am truly grateful. Now let me tell you how this crack cocaine game really works.

In the beginning, it starts out tasting like sugar, and at theend you will end up smelling like shit. Now go figure.

Again, I would like to thank each and every one of you who stood by me through it all. You know who you are, and for that, I am truly grateful.

Street Life and Prayer

Don't ask if God will heal you, just ask when.
—Geraldine Thomas

On November sixteenth twenty sixteen I will celebrate twenty years of sobriety, and I have not looked back that is only because of the Grace and Mercy of God, Amen!!!!

I had to also take full responsibility for my own actions before I was able to be healed, delivered, and set free.

If you ever find yourself searching the whole world over looking for love, just stop take a second and look within you will find it. Because your first love should be you Be Blessed.
—Geraldine Thomas

I contribute my healing, and recovery to these three Major factors.

- My Higher Power whom I choose to call my Lord and Savior Jesus Christ (Spirituality) 50%

- My Recovery which pointed out to me that "I did not have to use no matter what happens in my life". 25%

- My Psychological Therapist Who pointed out to me that it is ok to admit that my life had come unmanageable, and I was dealing with Insanity 25%

It took all three of these key points in my life to make me whole again, If one was missing I do not believe that I would have or could have made it through.

Geraldine
TRANSFERRED TO CAL STATE DOMINGUEZ HILLS

Los Angeles Southwest College

#LASCHANDLESBUSINESS

LASC

About the Author

Geraldine Thomas was born in Greenwood, Mississippi. She arrived in California in 1972 in search of a better life for her and her family. Along that journey, she was introduced to crack cocaine in 1980, which was one of the biggest mistakes she ever made in her entire life. She hopes this book will detour others from making the same mistake, and encourage them to seek God and recovery. Most of her addiction was alcohol. The last fifteen years of her addiction was mostly crack cocaine; therefore, the last fifteen years of her addiction was hell, not saying any of it was good. The reason she decided to write about her bottom—the lowest point in her life—is to let you know that crack cocaine or any type of drug will not only take control of your mind, it will take control of your body functions as well. "People, please don't allow this to happen to you because, believe me, once it has you in its grasp, it will not let go."

Today I attend a (CSU) (California State University,) my major is Psychology. The message in this book is "Don't let Your Past Predict Your Future". There is life after an Addiction. God Bless, Amen!!!!

www.ingramcontent.com/pod-product-compliance
Lightning Source LLC
Chambersburg PA
CBHW072005040426
42447CB00009B/1492